DISCARDED

Taxation

Other Books in the Issues on Trial Series:

Taxation

Sylvia Engdahl, Book Editor

GREENHAVEN PRESS
A part of Gale, Cengage Learning

GALE
CENGAGE Learning

Detroit • New York • San Francisco • New Haven, Conn • Waterville, Maine • London

Christine Nasso, *Publisher*
Elizabeth Des Chenes, *Managing Editor*

© 2011 Greenhaven Press, a part of Gale, Cengage Learning

For more information, contact:
Greenhaven Press
27500 Drake Rd.
Farmington Hills, MI 48331-3535
Or you can visit our Internet site at gale.cengage.com.

For product information and technology assistance, contact us at

Gale Customer Support, 1-800-877-4253
For permission to use material from this text or product, submit all requests online at www.cengage.com/permissions

Further permissions questions can be emailed to permissionrequest@cengage.com

Articles in Greenhaven Press anthologies are often edited for length to meet page requirements. In addition, original titles of these works are changed to clearly present the main thesis and to explicitly indicate the author's opinion. Every effort is made to ensure that Greenhaven Press accurately reflects the original intent of the authors. Every effort has been made to trace the owners of copyrighted material.

Cover Image © Wally McNamee/Corbis.

LIBRARY OF CONGRESS CATALOGING-IN-PUBLICATION DATA

Taxation / Sylvia Engdahl, book editor.
    p. cm. -- (Issues on trial)
    Includes bibliographical references and index.
    ISBN 978-0-7377-4492-7 (hardcover)
    1. Taxation--Law and legislation--United States--Juvenile literature. I. Engdahl, Sylvia.
    KF6289.85.T39 2010
    343.7304--dc22
                                                                            2010027862

Printed in the United States of America
1 2 3 4 5 6 7 14 13 12 11 10

Contents

Chapter 1: Social Security Taxes Must Be Paid Despite Religious Objections

Chapter 2: Failure to Pay Taxes Is Not a Crime If a Person Thought None Were Owed

Blackmun argues that Cheek's misinterpretation of the tax law had nothing to do with its complexity, that anyone of competent mentality would know its basic aspects, and that the Court's ruling will encourage taxpayers to adhere to foolish beliefs.

Chapter 3: States May Not Require Out-of-State Companies to Collect Sales Taxes

Upholding an earlier ruling, the Supreme Court decides that states cannot require out-of-state companies to collect sales taxes on sales made to their residents, and that companies without any physical presence in a state are to be considered out-of-state.

Chapter 4: Tribal Land That Has Been Owned by Non-Indians Is Not Tax-Exempt

Attorneys for the National Congress of American Indians argue that the state of New York originally purchased the Oneida land in violation of federal law and that although it passed to individual non-Indian owners, they were paid a fair market price when the Oneida bought it back; so it should regain its tax-exempt status.

Foreword

The U.S. courts have long served as a battleground for the most highly charged and contentious issues of the time. Divisive matters are often brought into the legal system by activists who feel strongly for their cause and demand an official resolution. Indeed, subjects that give rise to intense emotions or involve closely held religious or moral beliefs lay at the heart of the most polemical court rulings in history. One such case was *Brown v. Board of Education* (1954), which ended racial segregation in schools. Prior to *Brown*, the courts had held that blacks could be forced to use separate facilities as long as these facilities were equal to that of whites.

For years many groups had opposed segregation based on religious, moral, and legal grounds. Educators produced heartfelt testimony that segregated schooling greatly disadvantaged black children. They noted that in comparison to whites, blacks received a substandard education in deplorable conditions. Religious leaders such as Martin Luther King Jr. preached that the harsh treatment of blacks was immoral and unjust. Many involved in civil rights law, such as Thurgood Marshall, called for equal protection of all people under the law, as their study of the Constitution had indicated that segregation was illegal and un-American. Whatever their motivation for ending the practice, and despite the threats they received from segregationists, these ardent activists remained unwavering in their cause.

Those fighting against the integration of schools were mainly white southerners who did not believe that whites and blacks should intermingle. Blacks were subordinate to whites, they maintained, and society had to resist any attempt to break down strict color lines. Some white southerners charged that segregated schooling was *not* hindering blacks' education. For example, Virginia attorney general J. Lindsay Almond asserted, "With the help and the sympathy and the love and respect of the white people of the South, the colored man has risen under that educational process to a place of eminence and respect throughout the nation. It has served him well." So when the Supreme Court ruled against the segregationists in *Brown*, the South responded with vociferous cries of protest. Even government leaders criticized the decision. The governor of Arkansas, Orval Faubus, stated that he would not "be a party to any attempt to force acceptance of change to which the people are so overwhelmingly opposed." Indeed, resistance to integration was so great that when black students arrived at the formerly all-white Central High School in Arkansas, federal troops had to be dispatched to quell a threatening mob of protesters.

Nevertheless, the *Brown* decision was enforced and the South integrated its schools. In this instance, the Court, while not settling the issue to everyone's satisfaction, functioned as an instrument of progress by forcing a major social change. Historian David Halberstam observes that the *Brown* ruling "deprived segregationist practices of their moral legitimacy. . . . It was therefore perhaps the single most important moment of the decade, the moment that separated the old order from the new and helped create the tumultuous era just arriving." Considered one of the most important victories for civil rights, *Brown* paved the way for challenges to racial segregation in many areas, including on public buses and in restaurants.

In examining *Brown*, it becomes apparent that the courts play an influential role—and face an arduous challenge—in shaping the debate over emotionally charged social issues. Judges must balance competing interests, keeping in mind the high stakes and intense emotions on both sides. As exemplified by *Brown*, judicial decisions often upset the status quo and initiate significant changes in society. Greenhaven Press's Issues on Trial series captures the controversy surrounding influential court rulings and explores the social ramifications of such decisions from varying perspectives. Each anthology highlights one social issue—such as the death penalty, students' rights, or wartime civil liberties. Each volume then focuses on key historical and contemporary court cases that helped mold the issue as we know it today. The books include a compendium of primary sources—court rulings, dissents, and immediate reactions to the rulings—as well as secondary sources from experts in the field, people involved in the cases, legal analysts, and other commentators opining on the implications and legacy of the chosen cases. An annotated table of contents, an in-depth introduction, and prefaces that overview each case all provide context as readers delve into the topic at hand. To help students fully probe the subject, each volume contains book and periodical bibliographies, a comprehensive index, and a list of organizations to contact. With these features, the Issues on Trial series offers a well-rounded perspective on the courts' role in framing society's thorniest, most impassioned debates.

Introduction

No one likes to pay taxes, and certainly no one wants to pay higher taxes than the law requires. It is not surprising, therefore, that disputes over tax issues often arise. Tax law is an extremely complex area; even specially trained accountants and attorneys have great difficulty keeping up with what is, and is not, taxable under specific conditions. According to the Tax Foundation, as of 2005 the federal tax code and all Internal Revenue Service (IRS) regulations combined to total 9,097,000 words—and they have expanded significantly since then. This figure does not include state and local tax laws, which vary widely and add to the general confusion.

To be sure, the average taxpayer is not usually concerned with the ambiguities and uncertainties of the tax code; they affect mainly wealthy individuals and businesses. Nevertheless, tax laws are considered so complicated that ordinary citizens are not expected to understand them, and although tax evasion is a criminal offense, there is an exception to the general rule that "ignorance is no excuse." A person who was truly ignorant with regard to taxes due cannot be convicted of a crime for having failed to pay them, although he or she still must pay the amount owed, plus interest and penalties.

Tax questions are frequently taken to court, and some even reach the Supreme Court. In her book *The Majesty of the Law*, Supreme Court justice Sandra Day O'Connor writes, "If there is one fixed and invariant rule of law, it is that so long as there is more than one circuit [court], there will be more than one view of what the law is. . . . We find some mature, aging subject areas and some new, more fertile ones. We have, for example, seen a persistent drop in federal tax cases, from an average of more than eight a term from 1953 to 1965 to about four a term since then. Whether this reflects the Court's complete satisfaction with the current state of tax law or its utter despair, I cannot say."

The Supreme Court can consider only a small fraction of the vast number of cases appealed to it, and so it takes on only those that will have far-reaching impact on many people besides the individuals involved in the lower-court decision being reviewed. Often the question is whether a particular tax, or means of tax collection, is constitutional. With the exception of poll taxes, which were banned by the Twenty-fourth Amendment, states can collect whatever taxes their governments impose from their own citizens, as long as they do not violate the constitutional requirements of due process and equal protection. But federal taxes must be specifically authorized by the Constitution.

When the United States was formed, the new Constitution gave the federal government the power to tax, which it did not have under the Articles of Confederation. Article I, Section 8, states, "The Congress shall have Power to lay and collect Taxes, Duties, Imposts and Excises, to pay the Debts and provide for the common Defence and general Welfare of the United States; but all Duties, Imposts and Excises shall be uniform throughout the United States." This clause was sometimes held to conflict with the Tenth Amendment, which reserves to the states all powers not specifically granted to the federal government, for it does not clearly define what is meant by "general welfare." Throughout the nation's history there have been disputes over how broad an interpretation that term should be given, which the Supreme Court has resolved in different ways. As time passed, the Court tended to allow federal taxation for more and more purposes.

Until the last decade of the nineteenth century there was no federal income tax except for a short period during the Civil War. In 1894 the first one was imposed, but the next year, in *Pollock v. Farmers' Loan & Trust Company*, the Supreme Court ruled that it was unconstitutional on grounds it was a direct tax, which Article I, Section 2 of the Constitution requires to be apportioned among the states in proportion to their population. Congress responded by proposing the Sixteenth Amendment, ratified in 1913, which provides that "The Congress shall have power to lay and collect taxes on incomes, from whatever source derived, without apportionment among the several States, and without regard to any census or enumeration." Opponents challenged this, arguing that it violated the Fifth Amendment's prohibition against the government taking property without due process of law, but the Court rejected this argument in *Brushaber v. Union Pacific Railroad* (1916).

A few people today still claim the income tax is not legal; they maintain that the Sixteenth Amendment was not properly ratified or that some other technicality invalidates the tax law. Some of these tax protesters try to make money by selling books to the unsuspecting public or to cause trouble by tying up the courts with frivolous tax suits, while others have simply been misled. A search on the Internet for information about income taxes, and especially about the Sixteenth Amendment, brings up many sites containing plausible-sounding but erroneous statements, so it is wise to avoid any tax-advice site that is not run by a respected organization. Common sense should indicate that if there were any real question about the legality of the income tax, lawyers and judges would not be paying it themselves.

The fact that the income tax is constitutionally valid does not mean that there have been no legitimate suits connected with it. On the contrary, there have been—and still are—a great many concerning deductions and exemptions. Moreover, the Social Security Act of 1935, which imposed taxes for both unemployment compensation and old age insurance, was challenged on constitutional grounds and was upheld in two famous cases—*Steward Machine Company v. Davis* and *Helvering v. Davis*—decided by the Supreme Court on the same day in 1937. "It is too late today," wrote the Court in *Steward*, "for the argument to be heard with tolerance that in a crisis so ex-

treme the use of the moneys of the nation to relieve the unemployed and their dependents is a use for any purpose nar-
rower than the promotion of the general welfare." And in
Helvering, "The ill is all one . . . whether men are thrown out
of work because there is no longer work to do or because the
disabilities of age make them incapable of doing it. Rescue becomes necessary irrespective of the cause."

Today, similar issues are arising in regard to the health-
care reform bill passed by Congress in March 2010, which appears likely to be eventually considered by the Supreme Court.
There is extensive debate on the Internet as to whether the
mandatory health insurance portion of this law is constitutional, although the majority of legal experts believe that it is.
Opponents argue that there is nothing in the Constitution
that allows the government to make people buy something.
Under the new law, however, people who refuse to buy health
insurance would pay not a fine, but a tax—and there is now
ample precedent for the use of federal taxation to promote
the general welfare. A brief filed by the government in May
2010 stated that the law's provisions fall squarely within the
authority of Congress to levy taxes. It remains to be seen
whether the Court might affirm that reasoning, or might focus entirely on the federal power to regulate interstate commerce.

The interstate commerce clause of the Constitution is the
basis of many forms of federal taxation, such as various taxes
on businesses and on telecommunications. It is also frequently
cited by the Court in deciding questions involving state taxation that in one way or another crosses state lines. One such
question is whether states can require out-of-state sellers to
collect sales taxes from people who make purchases on the Internet, an issue that is becoming more and more controversial.
Many people are confused about this issue because they have
heard that Congress has put a moratorium on Internet taxes

that will last until 2014. However, the moratorium applies only to taxes on charges for Internet access, not for the purchase of goods.

Benjamin Franklin is believed to have been the first to say, "In this world nothing is certain but death and taxes." Whereas it is certainly sure that during each person's life there will be taxes to pay, the answers to legal questions about taxes are often not at all certain.

Chapter 1

Social Security Taxes Must Be Paid Despite Religious Objections

Case Overview

United States v. Lee (1982)

The Old-Order Amish live in close-knit rural communities and reject modern technology. They use horses and buggies rather than cars for transportation and wear traditional clothing. Most of them are farmers, but some practice crafts such as carpentry. This lifestyle is part of their religion, and it is very important to them. They are law-abiding, tax-paying citizens who keep to themselves and do not cause trouble, except when a law conflicts with their religious beliefs. Then they simply refuse to obey it.

One of their beliefs is that it is sinful not to take care of each other. The elderly and disabled among them are well provided for. The Amish consider this their own responsibility and do not accept help from outsiders or the government. For this reason, they believe it is wrong to buy insurance or participate in the Social Security program, which is called "insurance" although since the law says everyone must pay into it, the payments are actually a tax.

In 1955, Social Security, which had previously covered only employed workers, was extended to self-employed farmers. The Amish were unwilling to pay this tax, and the Internal Revenue Service (IRS) tried to collect by seizing money from their bank accounts. One farmer, Valentine Byler, closed his account to prevent its being taken, and he was arrested on a charge of contempt of court. The judge released him when he saw that Byler's refusal to pay was based on a firmly held religious conviction, but then the IRS seized three of the workhorses from his farm. There was an outcry from the public, leading first to a moratorium on collection of Social Security taxes from the Amish and eventually to the passage of a law by Congress that permanently exempted those who were self-employed, on condition that they waive all rights to future benefits.

However, the exemption did not apply to Amish employers or their employees. Edwin Lee, who employed Amish workers in his carpentry shop, paid under protest and in 1978 filed suit to prevent further IRS collection attempts, asking for a refund of the Social Security taxes he had already paid. The district court ruled in his favor on the grounds that forcing him to pay would violate his constitutional right to free exercise of his religion. The government appealed, so the case was taken up by the Supreme Court.

The government's attorney argued that if the Amish believed it was wrong to participate in Social Security, they did not have to accept any benefits from it. Lee's attorney argued that there was no need to force them to pay into the program because its sole purpose was to care for people in their old age, which the Amish did for themselves. He said that as a matter of principle they considered it a sin to pay, because it might later tempt some to accept the benefits to which it entitled them.

The Court unanimously ruled that no one can be excused from any tax except when explicitly exempted by Congress. It did not question the sincerity of the Amish people's religious beliefs, but it held that freedom of religion must be balanced with the common good. Limits can be placed on it when there is an overriding governmental interest, which in this case was the operation of the tax system—and that system could not function if people were permitted to avoid paying taxes because of their beliefs. Also, it said, allowing employers to opt out of Social Security would impose their religious faith on the employees (although the Amish normally do not employ outsiders).

Although the decision had gone against them, the Amish did not give up their fight for religious freedom. They petitioned Congress for expansion of their exemption from Social Security to include Amish employees working for Amish employers, and in 1988 the law was amended. Today, the only Amish required to pay into Social Security are the few who work for non-Amish employers.

> *"Granting an exemption from social security taxes to an employer operates to impose the employer's religious faith on the employees."*

Unanimous Opinion: Amish Employers Must Pay Social Security Taxes Despite Their Religious Objections

Warren E. Burger

Warren E. Burger was the chief justice of the United States from 1969 to 1986. He was a conservative who believed in a literal interpretation of the Constitution. In the following opinion that he wrote for the Court in United States v. Lee, *he explains that the district court ruled that Amish employers need not pay Social Security taxes because they believe it is sinful not to care for their own elderly and needy and their religion prohibits paying into the system as well as receiving benefits from it. He states that although Congress exempted self-employed Amish, this did not apply to employers or employees, so any exemption for them would have to be based on the constitutional right to religious freedom. However, Burger says, mandatory participation in Social Security is indispensable to the vitality of the system. There must be a balance between religious freedom and the common good. The obligation to pay Social Security is no different from the obligation to pay income tax, which the Amish do pay, and*

Warren E. Burger, unanimous opinion, *United States v. Lee*, U.S. Supreme Court, February 23, 1982. Reproduced by permission.

the tax system could not function if people were exempted on the basis of their religious beliefs. It must be uniformly applicable to all except when Congress explicitly provides otherwise.

Appellee, a member of the Old Order Amish, is a farmer and carpenter. From 1970 to 1977, appellee employed several other Amish to work on his farm and in his carpentry shop. He failed to file the quarterly social security tax returns required of employers, withhold social security tax from his employees, or pay the employer's share of social security taxes.

In 1978, the Internal Revenue Service assessed appellee in excess of $27,000 for unpaid employment taxes; he paid $91— the amount owed for the first quarter of 1973—and then sued in the United States District Court for the Western District of Pennsylvania for a refund, claiming that imposition of the social security taxes violated his First Amendment free exercise rights and those of his Amish employees.

The District Court held the statutes requiring appellee to pay social security and unemployment insurance taxes unconstitutional as applied. The court noted that the Amish believe it sinful not to provide for their own elderly and needy, and therefore are religiously opposed to the national social security system. The court also accepted appellee's contention that the Amish religion not only prohibits the acceptance of social security benefits, but also bars all contributions by Amish to the social security system. The District Court observed that, in light of their beliefs, Congress has accommodated self-employed Amish and self-employed members of other religious groups with similar beliefs by providing exemptions from social security taxes. The court's holding was based on both the exemption statute for the self-employed and the First Amendment; appellee and others "who fall within the carefully circumscribed definition provided in [this law] are relieved from paying the employer's share of [social security taxes], as it is an unconstitutional infringement upon the free exercise of their religion." . . .

Conflict Between Religion and Social Security Law

The exemption provided by [the law] is available only to self-employed individuals, and does not apply to employers or employees. Consequently, appellee and his employees are not within the express provisions of [that law]. Thus, any exemption from payment of the employer's share of social security taxes must come from a constitutionally required exemption.

The preliminary inquiry in determining the existence of a constitutionally required exemption is whether the payment of social security taxes and the receipt of benefits interferes with the free exercise rights of the Amish. The Amish believe that there is a religiously based obligation to provide for their fellow members the kind of assistance contemplated by the social security system. Although the Government does not challenge the sincerity of this belief, the Government does contend that payment of social security taxes will not threaten the integrity of the Amish religious belief or observance. It is not within "the judicial function and judicial competence," however, to determine whether appellee or the Government has the proper interpretation of the Amish faith; "[c]ourts are not arbiters of scriptural interpretation." *Thomas v. Review Bd. of Indian Employment Security Div.*, (1981). We therefore accept appellee's contention that both payment and receipt of social security benefits is forbidden by the Amish faith. Because the payment of the taxes or receipt of benefits violates Amish religious beliefs, compulsory participation in the social security system interferes with their free exercise rights.

The conclusion that there is a conflict between the Amish faith and the obligations imposed by the social security system is only the beginning, however, and not the end, of the inquiry. Not all burdens on religion are unconstitutional. The state may justify a limitation on religious liberty by showing that it is essential to accomplish an overriding governmental interest.

Tax Laws Must Be Uniformly Applied

Because the social security system is nationwide, the governmental interest is apparent. The social security system in the United States serves the public interest by providing a comprehensive insurance system with a variety of benefits available to all participants, with costs shared by employers and employees. The social security system is by far the largest domestic governmental program in the United States today, distributing approximately $11 billion monthly to 36 million Americans. The design of the system requires support by mandatory contributions from covered employers and employees. This mandatory participation is indispensable to the fiscal vitality of the social security system. "[W]idespread individual voluntary coverage under social security . . . would undermine the soundness of the social security program." Senate Rep. No. 404, 89th Congress (1965). Moreover, a comprehensive national social security system providing for voluntary participation would be almost a contradiction in terms, and difficult, if not impossible, to administer. Thus, the Government's interest in assuring mandatory and continuous participation in, and contribution to, the social security system is very high.

The remaining inquiry is whether accommodating the Amish belief will unduly interfere with fulfillment of the governmental interest. In *Braunfeld v. Brown*, (1961) this Court noted that "to make accommodation between the religious action and an exercise of state authority is a particularly delicate task . . . because resolution in favor of the State results in the choice to the individual of either abandoning his religious principle or facing . . . prosecution."

The difficulty in attempting to accommodate religious beliefs in the area of taxation is that "we are a cosmopolitan nation made up of people of almost every conceivable religious preference." *Braunfeld*. The Court has long recognized that balance must be struck between the values of the comprehensive social security system, which rests on a complex of actuarial factors, and the consequences of allowing religiously based exemptions. To maintain an organized society that guarantees religious freedom to a great variety of faiths requires that some religious practices yield to the common good. Religious beliefs can be accommodated, but there is a point at which accommodation would "radically restrict the operating latitude of the legislature." *Braunfeld.*

Unlike the situation presented in *Wisconsin v. Yoder,* , it would be difficult to accommodate the comprehensive social security system with myriad exceptions flowing from a wide variety of religious beliefs. The obligation to pay the social security tax initially is not fundamentally different from the obligation to pay income taxes; the difference—in theory at least—is that the social security tax revenues are segregated for use only in furtherance of the statutory program. There is no principled way, however, for purposes of this case, to distinguish between general taxes and those imposed under the Social Security Act. If, for example, a religious adherent believes war is a sin, and if a certain percentage of the federal budget can be identified as devoted to war-related activities, such individuals would have a similarly valid claim to be exempt from paying that percentage of the income tax. The tax system could not function if denominations were allowed to challenge the tax system because tax payments were spent in a manner that violates their religious belief. Because the broad public interest in maintaining a sound tax system is of such a high order, religious belief in conflict with the payment of taxes affords no basis for resisting the tax.

Congress has accommodated, to the extent compatible with a comprehensive national program, the practices of those who believe it a violation of their faith to participate in the social security system. Congress granted an exemption, on religious grounds, to self-employed Amish and others. Confining the exemption to the self-employed provided for a narrow category which was readily identifiable. Self-employed persons in a religious community having its own "welfare" system are distinguishable from the generality of wage earners employed by others.

Congress and the courts have been sensitive to the needs flowing from the Free Exercise Clause, but every person cannot be shielded from all the burdens incident to exercising every aspect of the right to practice religious beliefs. When followers of a particular sect enter into commercial activity as a matter of choice, the limits they accept on their own conduct as a matter of conscience and faith are not to be superimposed on the statutory schemes which are binding on others in that activity. Granting an exemption from social security taxes to an employer operates to impose the employer's religious faith on the employees. Congress drew a line in, exempting the self-employed Amish but not all persons working for an Amish employer. The tax imposed on employers to support the social security system must be uniformly applicable to all, except as Congress provides explicitly otherwise.

Accordingly, the judgment of the District Court is reversed, and the case is remanded for proceedings consistent with this opinion.

> *"The fact that the free exercise [of reli-*
> *gion] clause confers upon a community*
> *such as the Amish the right to main-*
> *tain the way of life that they choose . . .*
> *does not negate the obligations they*
> *have to the larger community."*

The Amish Should Be Required to Pay All Taxes

Lawrence G. Wallace and Justices of the Supreme Court

Lawrence G. Wallace was the attorney for the government in United States v. Lee. The following is his oral argument before the Supreme Court in the case. He states that although Congress did exempt self-employed Amish people from paying into Social Security, it did not intend any wider exemption, and employers still have to pay for their workers. He argues that this is a reasonable compromise with religious freedom. Other cases involving the free exercise of religion, he says, have involved more serious problems for the claimants, whereas if the Amish do not want to be in the Social Security program they simply do not have to accept benefits. In any case, contribution to Social Security is actually a tax, not insurance, and the Amish should be obliged to pay their share for the good of society. It should not depend on whether or not they withdraw money from the program.

*M*r. *Wallace*: Mr. Chief Justice, and may it please the Court, the Appellee in this case is a member of the old order Amish religious sect who employed other members of that

Lawrence G. Wallace and Justices of the Supreme Court, "Oral Argument, *United States v. Lee*," U.S. Supreme Court, November 2, 1981. Reproduced by permission.

sect on his farm and in his carpentry shop during the taxable years involved, 1970 through 1977. He did not withhold social security taxes from their wages or pay the employer's share of those taxes, and after an Internal Revenue Service assessment in 1978, he paid the taxes for one quarter of one year for an employee, and brought this suit for a refund, claiming that the tax as applied violated the free exercise clause of the First Amendment.

The basis for this claim is the belief of the old Amish sect to which he adhered that the members are to care for their aged, their sick, and their unemployed, and do not need any form of social welfare benefits from outside their religious community, and that it is a sin either to accept social security benefits or to pay the social security taxes. The District Court upheld his claim that the tax was unconstitutional as applied, and the United States appealed to this Court.

[Chief] Justice: At the time he made the first quarterly payment, Mr. Wallace, what were his alternatives?

Was he subject to a likely seizure or levying on his property?

Mr. Wallace: Well, the ordinary enforcement procedures to collect the taxes would be utilized, Mr. Chief Justice, but of course this case has been litigated, and none of those procedures have been put into effect. The case was tried on a stipulation, and counsel have agreed that the amount of taxes owing will be agreed upon should the United States prevail in this case.

Unidentified Justice: Well, but his act at that time in paying presumably did not compromise his religious beliefs because he had no choice, no real choice. If he wanted to continue his business, he had to yield to the government's demand.

Mr. Wallace: He at least was willing to make the payment. I can't really speak for whether that offended his religious beliefs. He made it under a claim of right to a refund, and perhaps that reconciled it with his belief. . . .

Self-Employed Amish Are Exempt

Unidentified Justice: Congress attempted to provide some relief for these people, did it not?

Mr. Wallace: It did provide an exemption from the self-employment tax, which we have referred to in our brief, but it was very careful in providing that exemption to limit it only to the self-employment tax, and the committee report specifies that the committee did not want to go beyond that and compromise the principle that social security contributions are not to be a voluntary matter beyond that narrow area.

Unidentified Justice: On the constitutional point, though, if he believes it is a sin for him to pay himself, apparently he also believes that it is a sin for him to pay for workers who are now working on his farm.

Mr. Wallace: Well, the claim does embrace the employees' share of the tax as well as the employer's share. Under the social security laws, both the employer and the employee are responsible for part of the tax, although as it happens in this case, since he did not withhold anything from the wages of the employees, he himself was responsible for the entire tax. . . .

Unidentified Justice:—Do you think the exemption with respect to self-employed Amish runs afoul of the establishment clause?

Mr. Wallace: We do not think so, Mr. Justice.

Unidentified Justice: Why?

Mr. Wallace: Although there is admittedly some tension with it, but we think it is a permissible accommodation of values, of religious values that the government can make under a number of this Court's cases that do permit some area of legislative discretion in accommodating religious beliefs with the general requirements of the law, and indeed, we think that the exemption could be extended to the employment taxes if Congress saw fit to do so.

Unidentified Justice: But at present, does it work this way, that the exemption applies to an individual, but if he engaged or employed ... how many people before the exemption would not be applicable?

Mr. Wallace: It is not applicable to the employment relationship at all.

Unidentified Justice: So if he had a single employee, the exemption would not be applicable?

Mr. Wallace: To the employment relationship.

Unidentified Justice: Yes.

Mr. Wallace: It is still applicable to his own self-employment.

Unidentified Justice: Of course.

Mr. Wallace: Even though it is not applicable to the wages that he pays to his employee.

Unidentified Justice: Mr. Wallace, perhaps you have stated it, but if so, I have missed it. What is the situation as to the employees here? Are they also old order Amish?

Mr. Wallace: The stipulation so states, although it doesn't say how many there are. The record just doesn't show that.

Unidentified Justice: Would the case be different if they were not?

Mr. Wallace: I think there would be less basis for the claim that there was a right to exclude them under the free exercise clause from social security coverage. Yes, Mr. Justice.

Unidentified Justice: Is it not true that some of the old order Amish have left the faith? . . .

Mr. Wallace:—The record does not show this.

The committee report which Congress issued and that it enacted the exemption for self-employment in 1965 did emphasize that the proposed exemption in their belief must be on the basis of individual choice to exclude all members of a religious group from social security coverage would not take account of the variances in individual beliefs within any religious groups, and would deny social security protection to those individuals who want it.

Among the old order Amish, for example, there have been some indications of a change in attitude towards social security, particularly among the younger people. Some members of the old order Amish who have become eligible for social security benefits have claimed the benefits. . . . However, nothing in the record of this case indicates anything of this kind.

Exceptions Not Made by Congress

[Chief] Justice: Even though you may not have made it as sharply as I am about to state it, I took the sum and substance of your position in the brief to be that the government of the United States can't run a nationwide program like tax collection or social security and one like this if there are these ad hoc exceptions, except as Congress explicitly makes them. Is that pretty close to your position?

Mr. Wallace: Yes, it is, Mr. Chief Justice.

Unidentified Justice: Well, then, how do you distinguish *Sherbert against Verner*, or the *Thomas* case of last year [1981]? . . .

Mr. Wallace: They involved much more serious problems for the claimant of the free exercise right, choosing between, in the *Sherbert* case, observance of one's Sabbath or one's economic livelihood, and in the *Thomas* case something very comparable, because of the loss of employment that was involved there, in order not to perform something that one believed could not be performed.

Here, the Amish, who do not want to be within the social security program, of course, do not have to accept benefits, and there is no indication that they believe that the furnishing of benefits to others in the national community who are covered by the program is in any way in conflict with their beliefs.

Their claim really is that there is, as they see it, an implication in their paying the tax that somehow they will become eligible for the benefits, and that indicates the sin of not planning to take care of their own community. But that is, with all respect to their belief, a construction that they choose to put on the payment. So far as Congress is concerned, this is just a generally applicable tax on a commercial relationship, and the employment relationship for engaging in commercial activity.

Unidentified Justice: Well, couldn't you say the same thing about *Thomas* last year?

Mr. Wallace: Well, in the *Thomas* case, he was performing work that was contrary to his religious belief, and by denying him unemployment compensation rights for giving up the job for that reason, there would be economic pressure on him to engage in work that is contrary to his religion.

Unidentified Justice: I take it, Mr. Wallace, you suggest here that they can pay the taxes; that doesn't stop them from continuing to support their own people.

Mr. Wallace: That is correct, Mr. Justice.

Unidentified Justice: Which is the distinction from *Sherbert* and *Thomas* that you make.

Mr. Wallace: It is the essence of the distinction that we make.

Unidentified Justice: They don't lose what Thomas and Verner, or Sherbert, or whoever it was, would have lost.

Mr. Wallace: Yes.

Unidentified Justice: But that suggests that in the scale of values the economic one is the top one rather than the religious belief of the particular claimant.

Mr. Wallace: Well, all religious beliefs as beliefs stand on the same footing under the Constitution.

A religious group might believe that it is a sin to pay any tax to secular authority, and that as a belief would stand on the same footing as the interpretation of social security tax payments that this group chooses to put on those payments, but that doesn't mean that there is a constitutional right to act on those beliefs and to refuse to pay the taxes that are levied on non-religious grounds generally in the community on the basis of commercial activities.

Unidentified Justice: Mr. Wallace, may I ask, is there anything in this record that suggests that the Amish would stop supporting their own people if they lost this case?

Mr. Wallace: Not at all. Not at all, Your Honor. . . .

[Chief] Justice: Is there anything to prevent them from having all of the social security or the other payments of this kind come back to a fund, the same kind of a fund that the Amish use to take care of their needy, in other words, so that it wouldn't come back to assist any individual except through the group operation?

Mr. Wallace: There is nothing in the law, Mr. Chief Justice, that would prevent a member of the Amish faith who is eligible to receive social security payments from receiving those payments and paying them over to a general fund in the community to care for members of the community. There may be an impediment to doing that in his religious faith, but there is nothing in the law that requires him to receive the benefits at all if he chooses not to receive the benefits. This is a right protected by the free enterprise clause.

Social Security Is a Tax, Not Insurance

Justice [Sandra Day O'Connor]: Mr. Wallace, I would like to ask you to identify what the compelling interest is of the government in requiring the Amish to pay into the social security system under the stipulated facts, which indicate that the Amish will not be withdrawing from the fund, and there is very little in the record that I can find that would focus on the real impact on the government of allowing them not to pay.

Mr. Wallace: Well, Justice O'Connor, we don't really, as we view the case, start from the standpoint that we need to show a compelling interest, but however one characterizes that, the interest is really one set forth in one of the classic opinions of Justice [Harlan] Stone, writing for this Court in one of the cases in Volume 301 of the U. S. Reports that upheld the constitutionality of the Social Security Act itself, and that established that the payments as Congress characterized them are taxes, and not insurance premiums, as is sometimes confused, and on Page 28 of our brief, we have set out the key paragraph of that opinion, and I would like to, if I may, turn our attention to it, because it seems to me to go to the heart of this case.

We don't really feel that the tax, that Congress's power to tax need be justified in terms of whether the Amish will be withdrawing benefits from the fund, the general fund that is collected, a taxes at that time Mr. Justice Stone said for the Court,

"is not an assessment of benefits."

"It is a means of distributing the burden of the cost of government."

"The only benefit to which a taxpayer is constitutionally entitled is that derived from his enjoyment of the privileges of living in an organized society, established and safeguarded by the devotion of taxes to public purposes."

"Any other view would preclude the levying of taxes except as they are used to compensate for the burden on those who pay them, and would involve the abandonment of the most fundamental principle of government, that it exists primarily to provide for the common good."

There are many contributions made in the community at large that contribute toward the maintenance of the way of life that the Amish have fashioned, and that under *Wisconsin against Yoder* they have a constitutional right to maintain as they choose to fashion it, but the fact is, it is not only through their efforts that that way of life can be maintained.

There are others in the community in general who are willing, for example, to train themselves in the advanced technology that is needed to defend the Country in today's world, and to protect the constitutional form of government which provides for the free exercise of religion, and others who are willing to serve in the armed forces, et cetera.

The fact that the free exercise clause confers upon a community such as the Amish the right to maintain the way of life that they choose to fashion for their community does not negate the obligations they have to the larger community, including the obligation to pay generally applicable taxes on commercial activities.

> *"The compelling state interest ... is to take care of older people, aged people, people that are disabled. [The Amish] do that themselves."*

The Amish Should Not Have to Participate in Something Against Their Religion

Francis X. Caiazza and Justices of the Supreme Court

Francis X. Caiazza was the attorney for the Amish in United States v. Lee. *The following viewpoint is excerpted from his oral argument before the Supreme Court in the case. He states that the Amish are a very religious people who live by their beliefs, and that they feel strongly about taking care of their own people instead of participating in government programs such as Social Security. They believe it is sinful not to rely on each other for care, and they fear that if they became eligible for Social Security payments, some Amish might accept them and thereby deny their faith. There is no need for them to participate, he argues, because the purpose of Social Security is to provide for the aged and the Amish have their own system for doing that. They do not object to paying taxes, but Social Security is called insurance rather than a tax, and the money goes into a separate fund. Caiazza acknowledges that there might be a problem if an Amish employer hired someone who was not Amish, but he says that does not happen because they are a very close-knit community.*

Francis X. Caiazza and Justices of the Supreme Court, "Oral Argument, *United States v. Lee*," U.S. Supreme Court, November 2, 1981. Reproduced by permission.

Mr. Caiazza: Mr. Chief Justice, and may it please the Court, after listening to the questions asked by the Court and the government's responses thereto, I think I would find it necessary really to depart from the prepared argument that I have made, because I feel that in arguing a question involving ... excuse me ... questions involving the freedom of religion certainly is a question that has to come from the feelings of the individual practitioner who is arguing the question.

Perhaps it is not permissible and proper for an attorney to become so personally involved with a particular issue. Maybe I have overstepped my bounds.

But I think the Court has to remember in this case that religion is something like beauty. Beauty is in the eyes of the beholder. I think that religion is the same thing. I think religion also has to be in the eyes of the believer. Religion means different things to different people. To some people, it may mean go to church on Sunday, or the Sabbath. Perhaps it has a social connotation to other people. But to some people the basic and the underlying principle of religion is the salvation of one's soul. That basically is what the Amish people are about.

It is pretty hard, really, to describe the Amish people without living with them, without going to see them, visiting their homes, talking to them, and I think by doing that you perhaps gain an insight into what the Amish people are about.

Unidentified Justice: In the *Thomas* case last spring [1981], didn't the Court say rather clearly that the judges can't get into the business of parsing out the doctrinal differences within a particular faith?

Mr. Caiazza: That is true, Mr. Chief Justice, but I think that is very applicable here, too, because I think in this particular case, what the government has said, that it is really a sin, they admit that it is a sin on behalf of the Amish people to pay into the system, but then what they go on to do is to say, well, that is not that great of a sin.

The Amish people, pure and simple, live by the Book of Timothy. The Book of Timothy, of course, paraphrased, says, if you don't take care of your own neighbors, you are worse than an infidel. That is the basic underlying principle of this particular case. That is the belief of the Amish people.

Amish Take Care of Their Own

Unidentified Justice: But isn't this whole social security system an organized way for a country of 200 million people to try to take care of their neighbors in an organized, institutionalized way?

Mr. Caiazza: That is true, but there are exceptions to that. As an example, Federal employees are not part of the social security system. They have their own system to take care of themselves. The Amish have their own system, which is the best system I have ever seen. They take care of their own. If they have tragedy, they are there to take care of them.

Unidentified Justice: Counsel, does the record show that any employees of these Amish were not Amish?

Mr. Caiazza:—No, all of the employees of Mr. Lee were members of the old order Amish. . . . Mr. Lee did not employ anybody who was not a member of his own sect.

Unidentified Justice: Mr. Caiazza, I gather from what you have said that if you lose this case, the Amish will not stop following their religious principle which, as you say, underlies this whole belief of taking care of their own.

Mr. Caiazza: They would continue to take care of their own. There is no question about that.

Unidentified Justice: Well, is there anything in the record at all that indicates that the payment of these taxes in any wise actually burdens their ability to take care of their own?

Mr. Caiazza: No, but I think it burdens their religious belief.

I think that is the issue.

Again, they do consider it a very serious sin to pay into the system, because what they are doing is denying their faith in the destiny of God.

They believe very frankly in the destiny of God, that God will—

Unidentified Justice: Does that suggest that it is a sin of such consequence that entirely without reference to their ability to take care of their own, it is an offense to their religion to pay—

Mr. Caiazza: Yes. I think . . . I feel very strongly about that. I think that once a particular group of individuals such as the Amish establish the fact that certain conduct is sinful, and that opinion is a sincere opinion such as the Amish people have, I don't think this Court or the government or anybody else can question the sincerity of that belief, and attach a sin to it as being mortal or venal in nature.

Unidentified Justice: Well, I didn't understand that the government was questioning at all, and certainly I do not, the sincerity of the belief.

Mr. Caiazza: They weren't questioning the sincerity of the belief, but they are saying the sin would simply be an incidental sin. It wouldn't be that great. . . .

Unidentified Justice: Does your case turn on the fact that they will not participate in the benefits, do you think?

Mr. Caiazza: They never . . . they do not participate in the benefits.

Unidentified Justice: Well, how can you guarantee that the employees might not at some time be non-members of the sect or might leave the sect before they become eligible for benefits?

Mr. Caiazza: They may leave the sect—

Unidentified Justice: Because there are people who leave the faith, are there not?

Mr. Caiazza: Yes, there are, very definitely. There are people that leave the faith.

But I think when you read Mr. Chief Justice Burger's opinion in the Yoder case, he alludes very clearly to the fact that the Amish children in the Yoder case had to be protected, that if they went to school beyond the eighth grade in that particular case, that they would be taught the ways of the world, and I think the same thing is true here as far as . . . the same reasoning applies as far as the social security is concerned.

If you make social security payments eligible, if you make the Amish people eligible to receive social security, that is there for them to receive, they may receive it and then deny their faith. That is what some of the older Amish people are concerned about, and I think rightly so.

Unidentified Justice: In other words, the taxpayer here is concerned about protecting his employees from the temptation of accepting welfare benefits later on?

Mr. Caiazza: Yes, I would think so, and I think that same reasoning applies in the Yoder case, as far as the temptation of students going to school beyond the eighth grade, and I think that is what the parents in Yoder were concerned about, and that is what the Amish employers are concerned about. . . .

The Purpose of Social Security

Unidentified Justice: You are not asking that the Amish people be given a preferred status under the First Amendment, are you?

Mr. Caiazza:—No, I am not. . . . I think we have to look at the compelling state interest, and you have to, I think, ask your question whether or not the state interest is justified. In my opinion, it is not justified in this particular case when we look at the Amish payment into the social security system.

Unidentified Justice: How do we decide whether a compelling state interest is justified or not? Do the nine of us just get in a room and flip a coin?

Mr. Caiazza: Well, I think you have to look at what the purpose of the social security system is. I think this is where the compelling state interest comes into play. The Amish people take care of themselves.

I think the compelling state interest is whether or not the Amish people as a group have the means to care for themselves. They have taken care of that compelling state interest themselves. I think that is what is important. They do have a system whereby they take care of their older people, they take care of their younger people, their sick people. . . .

The compelling state interest is, in my mind, anyway, as far as the Social Security Act is concerned, is to take care of older people, aged people, people that are disabled. They do that themselves. They have taken care of the compelling state interest themselves with their own actions and by their own beliefs based upon their belief in God and the destiny of God.

Unidentified Justice: I take it what you are saying to us is that they have their own little social security system and insurance within their own church organization.

Mr. Caiazza: They do.

Unidentified Justice: Well, now, what is to prevent them from having all the returns which came to individual Amish paid into that fund? Would that be regarded as tainted money, because it has gone into the government and back into the Amish fund?

Mr. Caiazza: I would think that it would be, because I think that what they are doing by paying into the system is denying their belief in the destiny of God. That is what is important.

Unidentified Justice: Well, when they get it back, haven't they washed that out?

Mr. Caiazza: They don't really take care of each other, though, by the use of moneys. What they do is, they take care of each other by the use of their physical labor.

Unidentified Justice: They must use money, too, I would think.

Mr. Caiazza: They definitely do, of course, need money, like anybody else, in order to subsist, but I think that the . . . I think that the important situation is the fact that when they do pay into the system, what they are doing is denying their belief that their future is guided by the destiny of God.

Unidentified Justice: Mr. Caiazza, I am not clear yet whether you would take the same position you are taking if the employees were not Amish. Would it still be a sin to pay the tax, the social security tax? . . .

Mr. Caiazza: I think it would be a sin to pay the employer's half. It would not be a sin to pay the employee's half. As a matter of practicality, the Amish people just employ old Amish. They are a very close-knit community.

Unidentified Justice: But it would be your position that even if non-Amish employees were hired, that it would still constitute a problem?

Mr. Caiazza: Yes, it would.

Unidentified Justice: Now, would that not in effect mean that the government is running into establishment clause problems, and is in effect favoring the Amish and enabling them to compete in a manner that other people don't have to contend with?

Mr. Caiazza: Of course, there is a lot of tension between the establishment clause and the free exercise clause. I think when you consider the number of Amish people there are in this country, I think when you consider their general practices of Amish people working together and not employing members who are not members of the old order Amish, I don't think you really run into that question. If the situation did arise whereby an Amishman did hire an individual who was not a member of the Amish faith, yes, you would have a problem, but as a matter of practicality, that just does not come up because they are a very close community. They stay within their own bounds. . . .

Unidentified Justice: Counsel, many people think it is immoral to fund abortions from the Medicaid component of social security. Do you think they would have the same right that you are contending for here today?

Mr. Caiazza: Certainly they would have the same right to present their case. I haven't really thought about that in great detail. . . . I would hate to comment myself on what direction I would go in, but I would certainly think that they would have the right to present that issue, but again I think we get back to the compelling state interest.

Unidentified Justice: It would have a devastating effect on the social security tax, at least on the Medicaid component, if that view prevailed, wouldn't it?

Mr. Caiazza: Yes, sir. I realize that probably the greatest problem with this case is the fact that we are dealing with taxes. Of course, social security, I feel, in my mind, is more of an insurance than a tax. Of course, the name of the Act is the Federal Insurance Contribution Act. It is set up in a trust fund, and I think that the moneys are distributed basically the same way that insurance carriers distribute annuity funds. . . .

Unidentified Justice: Well, then, just to make it clear, you do take the position that if social security were financed out of general revenues, that you could make the same argument about the regular income tax?

Mr. Caiazza: I don't really think so. I think if social security was financed out of general revenues, I think your compelling state interest would be different. Social security funds are set aside.

Many of the Amish people are against many social welfare programs that are really financed by general revenues which come from income tax which they pay, but I don't think that it would be fair or proper to place on the government the responsibility to distinguish where everybody's tax dollar goes on a dollar by dollar basis. That is not true as far as the Social Security Act is concerned. The money goes into the system and is paid out of the system.

Unidentified Justice: You are saying the legal question will be different, but would it not be equally a sin for the Amish to pay income tax if the income tax were used to finance welfare programs that would be available to some members—

Mr. Caiazza: Yes. . . . —It would be a sin, but I think you get back again to the compelling state interest.

Unidentified Justice: Then you are saying the governmental interest would override.

Mr. Caiazza: It would override it.

"The Amish believe that, if the church is faithful to its calling, commercial insurance and government welfare programs are unnecessary."

The Amish Believe That Participation in Welfare or Insurance Programs Is Unnecessary

Carl Watner

Carl Watner, a historian of libertarian studies, is the publisher and editor of the Voluntaryist *newsletter and the author of several books. In the following article he explains the views of the Amish, who live in a traditional way apart from modern civilization. The Amish take care of their own people, he says, and do not rely on outsiders or the government for help. They are law-abiding citizens except when it conflicts with their religion, but when it does, they will not compromise their beliefs. They pay taxes, but Social Security has always been described by the government as insurance. The Amish believe that it is wrong to rely on insurance instead of taking the responsibility of caring for each other, so they refused to pay Social Security. In 1965 Congress exempted those who were self-employed, but Amish employers were still required to pay for their workers. One of them, Edwin Lee, took the issue to court, and the lower court ruled that requiring him to pay was unconstitutional because it would interfere with the free exercise of his religion. The Supreme*

Carl Watner, "By Their Fruits Ye Shall Know Them: Voluntaryism and the Old Order Amish," in *I Must Speak Out*, Fox & Wilkes, 1999, pp. 268–74. Copyright © 1999 by Carl Watner. Reproduced by permission.

Court, however, overruled this decision on the grounds that the tax system could not function if there were any exemptions other than those specified by Congress.

The traditional Amish values—"obedience, hard work, responsibility, and integrity"—are all reinforced by the yielding of the individual to the consensus of the community. If the individual refuses to compromise, he is ostracized socially and boycotted economically.

Yet for those who stay, there is the deep-seated assurance that they will be taken care of for life, providing they make every effort to take care of themselves. The Amish believe that, if the church is faithful to its calling, commercial insurance and government welfare programs are unnecessary. Their ethic of mutual assistance flows from the Biblical emphasis on charity, taking care of one's own, and from the spirit of *Gelassenheit*, "with its doctrine of humility, self-sacrifice, self-denial, and service to others." By not having to rely on outsiders or the state for help, the mutual aid system of the Amish permits them to remain aloof and separate from the outside world. Mutual aid far exceeds the romanticized barn raisings we have read about or seen in the movies. "Harvesting, quilting, births, weddings, and funerals require the help of many hands. The habits of care encompass responses to all sorts of disasters—drought, disease, death, injury, bankruptcy, and medical emergency. The community springs into action in these moments of despair—articulating the deepest sentiments of Amish life. Shunning governmental assistance and commercial insurance, the Amish system of mutual aid marks their independence as well as their profound commitment to a humane system of social security at every turn." . . .

The Amish View of the State

"Centuries of persecution have resulted in an almost instinctive distrust of government. The Amish realize that the hand that feeds you also controls you." The Amish see the state as the embodiment of force, since the army and police are the most essential parts of government. Nevertheless, the Amish are law-abiding, tax-paying citizens until the laws of man conflict with the laws of God. Then they can be stubborn as a mule, refusing to compromise deeply-held beliefs, and will respectfully take a stand opposing government, even if it means prosecution, fines, imprisonment, or death. The Amish maintain a very apolitical or "courteous disregard for the affairs of state." They apply this strategy of non-involvement to such questions as whether a Christian should vote, serve on a jury, or hold public office. Most Amishmen believe that if they do not help elect or vote for government officials, the latter are not their representatives, and therefore they are not responsible for what these office-holding wielders of the sword do. . . .

The Amish do believe in paying their taxes, and they have never opposed the payment of real estate, property, school, sales, county, or federal and state income taxes. However, most Amishmen would agree that after they pay their taxes, the tax is no longer their money. Hence they have no responsibility for how the government spends the money, nor do they consider it their responsibility to tell the government how it should be used. If the Amish hold these attitudes, then why did they oppose payment of taxes to the Old Age, Survivors and Disability Insurance (Social Security) program? Why didn't they pay their taxes and refuse the benefits offered by the government?

The Amish vs. Social Security

The answer to this question is two-fold. First, as already mentioned, the Amish are adamantly opposed to participation in all commercial and governmental insurance schemes, and are just as adamant against receiving public welfare assistance. Since the very beginning of its propaganda on behalf of Social Security, the federal government has described it as an insurance program. However mistaken this nomenclature might be, the Amish accepted it at face value, and consequently viewed Social Security as the government portrayed it. Thus to the Amish, they were not refusing to pay a tax, but rather opposed to participating in an insurance program. The second reason the Amish opposed Social Security was that Amish leaders "feared that if their members paid Social Security, future generations would be unable to resist receiving the benefits for which they had already paid. Payment of taxes would be seen as participation in the system, and if paying was allowed, then how could receiving benefits be prohibited?"

The Amish first encountered the Social Security question in 1955, when it was extended to cover self-employed farmers. The Amish used many dodges to avoid complicity with the program. Some simply did not pay; others allowed the IRS [Internal Revenue Service] to seize money from their bank accounts. Valentine Y. Byler, an Amish farmer from New Wilmington, Penn., was one of the hardliners, who closed his bank account in order to forestall IRS collection. In June 1959, the IRS filed a lien against Byler's horses for nonpayment of his Social Security taxes. In July 1960, the IRS served him with a summons to appear in court to defend his actions. When he failed to honor the summons, he was seized by government agents in August 1960, and taken to the US District Court in Pittsburgh to answer charges of contempt. The charges were lifted when the judge realized that Byler was refusing to pay his Social Security taxes because of a firmly-held religious conviction. Finally, on April 18, 1961 Byler received national attention when IRS agents came onto his farm and seized three of his work horses for nonpayment of his taxes.

The resulting furor led to a temporary moratorium on the collection of Social Security taxes from the Amish. In September 1961, Mortimer Caplan, Commissioner of the IRS, met with a group of Amish bishops in hopes of resolving the stalemate. The Amish refused to contribute to Social Security in any way, but finally agreed to initiate a lawsuit that would determine whether or not their sect was entitled to an exemption based upon the fact that forced participation in Social Security was a violation of their religious freedom. In April 1962, Byler filed the promised suit, but soon he and the Amish bishops had second thoughts, realizing that "going to court violated their religious beliefs." The suit was withdrawn in January 1963. Meanwhile the Amish bishops collected signatures and petitioned their representatives in Congress, pressing their case for a legislative exemption, which finally passed in 1965.

The exemption applied to self-employed workers who were members of a religious sect continually in existence since 1950, and "with established tenets opposed to accepting the benefits of any private or public retirement plan or life, disability, or health insurance." Each person must certify on IRS exemption form No. 4029 that he or she is conscientiously opposed to receiving government benefits such as Social Security and Medicare, "and must do so before becoming entitled to receive" those benefits. Furthermore, the worker must waive "all rights to future benefits for self and dependents under those programs." This government-granted exemption did not cover Amish employees working for Amish or non-Amish employers, so that at least some Amishmen were still liable for the tax. In addition, since the Social Security tax was both paid by employees and employers, some Amish employers, although not responsible for Social Security tax on their own earnings from self-employment, were still liable for their employer's share of the Social Security tax on the earnings of their employees (whether Amish or not). This oversight led to the next stage in the struggle involving the Amish and Social Security.

United States v. Lee

In the case of *United States v. Lee* the Supreme Court decided, in 1982, that the burden on an Amish employer, Edwin Lee, was not unconstitutional "since the state's overriding interest in maintaining the nationwide Social Security system justified the limitation on religious liberty." Between 1970 and 1977, Edwin Lee employed Amish workers in his carpentry shop and on his farm. He objected to being forced to contribute the employer's share of the Social Security tax on these employees because of the sect's religious scruples about participation in the Social Security program. In 1978, Lee sued for an injunction blocking IRS collection efforts and asked for a refund of the amount of Social Security tax he had actually paid on these workers. The federal district court granted the injunction and refund on the basis that "requiring Lee to participate in Social Security and pay the employer tax for his workers" would be a violation of his rights to the free exercise of his religion guaranteed in the First Amendment to the U.S. Constitution.

On appeal by the government, the Supreme Court overruled the lower court's decision, and while granting Lee's religious freedom was violated, it held that there were more important interests at stake. The majority opinion of the Court demonstrated concern with a number of issues. First, the Court noted that the 1965 Congressional exemption applied only to self-employed individuals, not to employees or employers. Second, the Court agreed that the forced payment of taxes to or receipt of benefits from the Social Security program did violate the Amish religious beliefs and did, in fact, interfere with their freedom of religion. But the Court noted, that "Not all burdens on religion are unconstitutional. . . . [T]he State may justify a limitation on religious liberty by showing that it is essential to accomplish an overriding governmental interest."

The court's main concern was the smooth functioning of the tax system. This became apparent in its discussion of taxation and religious freedom. The Court observed that there was no fundamental difference between paying federal income taxes and paying the Social Security tax. Both were forced contributions to the government's treasury. As the Court said, "There is no principled way, however, for purposes of this case, to distinguish between general taxes and those imposed under the Social Security Act. If, for example, a religious adherent believes war is a sin, and if a certain percentage of the federal budget can be identified as devoted to war-related activities, such individuals would have a similarly valid claim to be exempt from paying that percentage of the income tax. The tax system could not function if denominations were allowed to challenge the tax system because tax payments were spent in a manner that violates their religious belief. . . . Because the broad public interest in maintaining a sound tax system is of such a high order, religious belief in conflict with the payment of taxes affords no basis for resisting the tax."

Congressional Exemption

Having lost the case, the Amish probably concluded that it was a lawsuit "that should never have been brought." For one thing it violated the Amish injunction against initiating court cases. For another, it left the Amish no constitutional route to make any further challenges. Their only option was to lobby and petition for an amendment to the original Congressional exemption. In 1988, they succeeded in expanding the 1965 exemption to "include Amish employees working for Amish employers exempting both from the tax." Consequently the only Amish who are currently liable for any Social Security tax payments are those working for non-Amish employers. "Although relatively small in number, these persons pay into the system but generally do not accept its benefits."

> *"In no uncertain terms, the Supreme Court said that because the government needs the money it is permissible to violate the constitutional rights of a citizen."*

The Court's Ruling Disregarded Constitutional Limits on Government Power

Daniel J. Pilla

Daniel J. Pilla is a tax litigation consultant and author of many books on taxation. In the following viewpoint he argues that the Supreme Court has made decisions that erode citizens' liberties by taking a role that the Constitution gives to Congress rather than the courts. Especially in tax cases, he says, the Court generally disregards limits on government power—however, when it ruled that federal judges need not contribute to Social Security, it stuck to what the Constitution says about not reducing their compensation while they are in office. This was the opposite of what it decided in the case of whether the Amish had to pay Social Security taxes, which in Pilla's opinion was a violation of their religious liberty. He declares that the Court's different treatment of the two cases shows a disregard of their duty to protect ordinary citizens' constitutional rights.

As the highest court in the land, the Supreme Court is intended to be the guardian of liberty. In *Federalist* No. 78, Alexander Hamilton referred to the judicial branch as the

Daniel J. Pilla, "Guardians of the Constitution or Watching Out for Their Own?" *The Freeman*, vol. 47, September 1997. Copyright © 1997 Foundation for Economic Education, Incorporated. www.thefreemanonline.org. All rights reserved. Reproduced by permission.

"citadel of the public justice and the public security." The Supreme Court, indeed the entire judicial branch of government under Article III [of the U.S. Constitution], was set up as an element of government independent of the other two. The founders knew that an independent judiciary was critical to maintaining liberty.

The legislative powers are vested in Congress under Article I. They are intended to pass laws necessary to carry out the terms of the Constitution as set forth in the preamble. The executive department under Article II possesses the power to carry out the legitimate functions of government and to control the armed forces. Described in modern terms, the Supreme Court, on the other hand, is intended to function as a goalie. It is to "kick out" any legislative or executive act that infringes the plain language of the Constitution.

Regarding legislation, the court is to do nothing more than compare the language of the statute with that of the Constitution to see whether the former comports with the latter. If so, the statute is legitimate and enforceable. If not, the statute is void under the terms of Article VI. It is to be struck down.

Of the language describing the three branches of government, Article III is by far the most succinct. The founders dedicated ten sections in Article I to explain the function of the legislative branch and four lengthy sections in Article II to describe the executive. Article III has just three short sections. These, combined with the concise language of Article VI, make it clear that the court has no power to make laws or negate specific Constitutional provisions or protections. The court is a goalie, not a forward. Goalies do not score.

For decades since the 1930s, however, the Supreme Court has taken an activist role. Too many of its decisions fall outside the scope of judicial review; they have the character of legislation. As a result, our constitutional liberties have eroded substantially, while at the same time the power and reach of the federal government has been extended to all areas of our private lives in absolute disregard of the limitations set forth in the Constitution.

The Judges Go to Court

This is particularly true in tax cases. Whereas the Constitution plainly confines the power of government in several important areas, virtually all the limits have been declared invalid as they relate to the Internal Revenue Service. But when the power of taxation imposes upon the rights of federal judges, the courts are quick to protect their own.

Consider the case of Judge Terry J. Hatter and 15 of his colleagues. Hatter and the others are federal judges all appointed to the bench sometime before January 1983. Like most federal employees at the time, they were not subject to the Social Security tax laws. Rather, they enjoyed their own pension under the Civil Service Retirement System.

Beginning in 1982, however, Congress changed the law. To address the growing concerns over the solvency of Social Security, two major tax laws were passed in 1982 and 1983. The first was the Tax Equity and Fiscal Responsibility Act of 1982. The second was the Social Security Amendments of 1983. The first made the hospital insurance portion of Social Security applicable to federal employees, including judges, effective January 1, 1983. The second made the old age and survivors disability portion—the bulk of Social Security taxes—applicable to federal employees, including judges, effective January 1, 1984.

As a result of being brought within the pale of the Social Security tax scheme by these two laws, Hatter and his brethren sued the federal government claiming a violation of their constitutional rights. How can imposing income taxes on judges possibly violate the Constitution? If we citizens have to pay taxes, why not federal judges? The answer lies within the language of Article III, section 1, which holds that the compensation of federal judges "shall not be diminished during their Continuance in Office." Hatter argued that the imposition of the tax after he took office violated that clause.

Hamilton described the purpose of the compensation clause as being essential to protecting the separation of powers. He wrote in *Federalist* No. 79 that, "in the general course of human nature, a power over a man's subsistence amounts to a power over his will." Nothing could more aptly describe the power of the purse. Our founders knew that if the judiciary was to remain independent of Congress and the executive department, their compensation would have to be beyond their tampering.

The language of Article III has always been broadly construed to prohibit any diminution in compensation during a judge's tenure. Indeed, a similar suit was brought by federal judges in the years immediately following the adoption of the income tax in 1913. The case of *Evans v. Gore* found its way to the Supreme Court, where it was held that the prohibition contained no exception for "diminution by taxation." Judges appointed to the bench after the tax took effect were subject to it. However, those who held office before the tax was enacted were held exempt.

In the case of *Hatter v. United States*, the U.S. Court of Appeals reached the same conclusion. The Supreme Court unceremoniously affirmed the ruling.

Some Are More Equal than Others

When the question of the constitutionality of a federal tax relates to a federal judge, the courts seem to have no difficulty ascertaining the plain language of the Constitution and applying it to the statute. When it is found that the Constitution prohibits the legislative act prescribed by the statute, the courts have no difficulty slapping down the infringement.

But let us contrast that with a case involving a private citizen and his equally compelling constitutional argument. That case is *United States v. Lee* (1982). The case involved precisely the same Social Security laws. The fundamental difference is that Lee was not a federal judge but a self-employed farmer and carpenter. He was a member of the Old Order Amish and employed several persons in his business. Lee's complaint grew not from the compensation clause but from the free-exercise clause of the First Amendment.

Because the Amish are religiously opposed to the kinds of benefits offered by Social Security, Lee did not participate in the system. He neither paid into it nor expected to draw from it.

Prior to the Social Security amendments of 1982 and 1983, the law expressly provided that Lee and those of his religious community were not required to withhold Social Security taxes from their employees or pay the matching funds. The new law, however, extended the tax obligation to wages paid by employers to employees, even if the employees were not liable for the tax themselves. As a result, Lee found himself faced with the duty to pay matching funds for a tax that he was plainly opposed to on religious grounds and that he was exempt from paying under prior law.

Lee opted to stick to his religious principles and did not pay the taxes. He was assessed several thousand dollars by the IRS, and after paying a portion of the tax, he sued for a refund. After initial success, Lee found himself before the Supreme Court.

The First Amendment, of course, expressly states that Congress "shall make no law" respecting an establishment of religion or "prohibiting the free exercise thereof." In its opinion, the Supreme Court found that because of the Amish faith, "compulsory participation in the social security system interferes with [Lee's] free exercise rights" under the First Amendment. This is the conclusion a liberty-minded person would have hoped the court would reach. Unfortunately, its reasoning did not end there. Chief Justice Warren Burger went on to explain that the courts must strike a "balance" between the rights of the citizen and an "overriding" governmental interest. He reasoned that when the government could show such an "overriding interest," it could infringe the plain and clear constitutional rights of the citizen.

The Court held that Lee must be forced to participate in the Social Security program despite its finding that this expressly violated his First Amendment rights. It rationalized the infringement by citing the government's "overriding interest" in collecting taxes and stating that "mandatory participation is indispensable to the fiscal vitality of the social security program." Citing the questionable financial soundness of the system, Chief Justice Burger observed that "widespread individual voluntary coverage under social security . . . would undermine the soundness of the social security program."

In no uncertain terms, the Supreme Court said that because the government needs the money it is permissible to violate the constitutional rights of a citizen. Thus, the only "overriding governmental interest" involved in the Lee case is financial.

In concluding, Chief Justice Burger reasoned that religious beliefs "can be accommodated, but there is a point at which accommodation would radically restrict the operating latitude of the legislature." The Supreme Court was saying that Congress must have free rein—absolute freedom—to pass laws. Religious and presumably other constitutional rights cannot be permitted to exist if they threaten the government's ability to do so.

Note how far this logic is removed from the model set forth by Hamilton in *Federalist* No. 78. In affirming the court's power of judicial review, Hamilton said, "If there should happen to be an irreconcilable variance between the two [the Constitution and a legislative act], that which has the superior obligation and validity ought, of course, to be preferred; or, in other words, the Constitution ought to be preferred to the statute."

From beginning to end, the Bill of Rights places express restrictions on government's ability to pass laws. Without such restrictions, this government is no better than any dictatorship that has ever existed. Those restrictions directly and simply forbid the invasion of individual rights by a government eager to pass laws that infringe our liberty. Yet the Supreme Court in *Lee* held that the limitations are placed on the individual, not on government. Individual rights can be "accommodated," but only if they do not stand in the way of some legislative goal. With such a test, there is literally nothing the federal government cannot do in the name of some "overriding interest."

Are Rights to Be Balanced?

Where in the First Amendment does it say that your religious liberty is dependent upon a "balancing" test? Where does it say that Congress should "accommodate" those rights, but only if they do not interfere with its own right to legislate? Just as the Supreme Court noted in *Evans* regarding Article III and the compensation clause, there are "no excepting words" in the First Amendment. The right is absolute and is expressly intended to limit Congress in its zeal to pass restrictive laws. What other purpose is possibly served by the plain language "Congress shall make no law"?

When it comes to the rights of the average citizen, the courts have abandoned a strict reading of the plain language in favor of judicial creativity designed specifically to achieve the predetermined goal of getting into your pocket. . . .

How is it that a federal judge's constitutional rights are more sacred than those of the average citizen? Judges are charged with the sacred duty of protecting the rights of all citizens from encroachment by government. Yet, as we have seen, they embrace that duty when it comes to their own liberty and tear it to shreds when it would cloak the liberty of the average man.

What has happened to our courts? They have caused our priceless constitutional system of law and limited government to deteriorate. What system of taxation or social program is so important that we should sacrifice our precious liberty to save it?

CHAPTER *2*

Failure to Pay Taxes Is Not a Crime If a Person Thought None Were Owed

Case Overview

Cheek v. United States (1991)

All Americans know that unless their income is very low, they must pay a federal tax on it—or do they? Actually, a few people claim not to be aware of that fact. There are many tax protesters who say that the government does not have the legal power to impose income taxes, some of whom honestly believe it and try to convince others. This is different from just disagreeing with the tax laws or the purposes for which taxes are used. There is no legal excuse for failing to pay because of mere disagreement, but surprisingly, in the case of tax law—unlike other areas of law—allowances are made for ignorance.

Tax evasion is a crime for which people can be sent to prison. Therefore, anyone charged with it is entitled to a jury trial. From 1980 to 1986 an airline pilot named John Cheek failed to pay any income tax. At his trial he testified that he had attended seminars by tax protesters that had caused him to believe that the income tax was unconstitutional and that his wages from American Airlines did not constitute income under the internal revenue laws.

Only when a defendant's failure to pay is "willful"—in other words, deliberate—can he or she be convicted of tax evasion. Thus the question for the jury was whether Cheek had willfully violated the law or had really thought that it did not apply to him. The jury was confused about how to make this determination, so they asked the judge for clarification. The judge told them that an "honest but unreasonable belief is not a defense, and does not negate willfulness." He also said that if they concluded that Cheek's beliefs were not reasonable, there was no basis for acquitting him.

The jury decided that it was unreasonable for someone intelligent enough to be employed as an airline pilot to believe that wages are not income. Cheek was therefore convicted. His conviction was upheld by the Court of Appeals, after which the Supreme Court agreed to review his case. The Court ruled seven to two that a defendant's honest belief that wages are not taxable may be grounds for negating the willfulness requirement—even if that is an unreasonable belief. Such a position indicates mere ignorance. And although ignorance is no excuse in the case of most laws, under tax laws it is permitted because those laws are so complex that average citizens cannot be expected to fully understand them.

This decision amazed many observers, some of whom, including the dissenting justices, felt that it would encourage tax evaders to claim unreasonable beliefs about the law in the hope of convincing a jury that they honestly held them. It is extremely likely, however, that the jury will not be convinced. The Supreme Court's ruling in John Cheek's favor did not mean that he escaped punishment. On the contrary, because the judge's instructions to the jury had been erroneous, his case was remanded for retrial. At his second trial the jury rejected his claim that he had believed wages were not taxable. He was again convicted, and when the conviction was upheld by the U.S. Court of Appeals, the Supreme Court denied his petition for another review. He was sentenced to a year and a day in prison and payment of back taxes.

It is important to realize that even a person's sincere belief that he or she owes no income tax does not get that person out of paying it—at most, it is a defense against being convicted of a felony. The tax still must be paid after an acquittal, with interest and penalties added. So the Court's ruling did not create an opportunity to avoid having to pay.

"It was error for the court to instruct the jury that petitioner's asserted beliefs that . . . he was not a taxpayer within the meaning of the Internal Revenue Code should not be considered."

Majority Opinion: A Sincere Belief That No Income Tax Is Owed Need Not Be Reasonable

Byron R. White

Byron R. White was a justice of the Supreme Court from 1962 to 1993. In the following opinion for the Court in Cheek v. United States, *he states that John Cheek claimed that he had failed to pay income tax because he had followed the advice of a group that told him the federal tax system is unconstitutional and that the Sixteenth Amendment did not authorize a tax on wages and salaries, but only on profits. At Cheek's trial the judge had instructed the jury that an objectively reasonable good-faith misunderstanding of the law was a defense against criminal liability for failure to pay, but mere disagreement with the law was not. Cheek appealed his conviction because he believed the judge should not have said a belief must be reasonable to qualify as a defense. White explains that tax offenses receive special treatment, allowing for ignorance, because of the complexity of the tax law. He says that in order to convict a defendant, the government must prove that he willfully violated the law, which it*

Byron R. White, majority opinion, *Cheek v. United States*, U.S. Supreme Court, January 8, 1991. Reproduced by permission.

cannot do if the jury believes his claim that he did not know what it requires. The trial judge was wrong, White says, to tell the jury that a misunderstanding must be reasonable. A claim that the law is unconstitutional, on the other hand, is not a defense because to draw that conclusion Cheek would have to be aware of the provisions he disagreed with.

Petitioner John L. Cheek has been a pilot for American Airlines since 1973. He filed federal income tax returns through 1979, but thereafter ceased to file returns. He also claimed an increasing number of withholding allowances—eventually claiming 60 allowances by mid-1980—and for the years 1981 to 1984 indicated on his W-4 forms that he was exempt from federal income taxes. In 1983, petitioner unsuccessfully sought a refund of all tax withheld by his employer in 1982. Petitioner's income during this period at all times far exceeded the minimum necessary to trigger the statutory filing requirement.

As a result of his activities, petitioner was indicted for 10 violations of federal law. . . . The tax offenses with which petitioner was charged are specific intent crimes that require the defendant to have acted willfully.

At trial, the evidence established that, between 1982 and 1986, petitioner was involved in at least four civil cases that challenged various aspects of the federal income tax system. In all four of those cases, the plaintiffs were informed by the courts that many of their arguments, including that they were not taxpayers within the meaning of the tax laws, that wages are not income, that the Sixteenth Amendment does not authorize the imposition of an income tax on individuals, and that the Sixteenth Amendment is unenforceable, were frivolous or had been repeatedly rejected by the courts. During this time period, petitioner also attended at least two criminal trials of persons charged with tax offenses. In addition, there was evidence that, in 1980 or 1981, an attorney had advised Cheek that the courts had rejected as frivolous the claim that wages are not income.

Cheek represented himself at trial and testified in his defense. He admitted that he had not filed personal income tax returns during the years in question. He testified that, as early as 1978, he had begun attending seminars sponsored by, and following the advice of, a group that believes, among other things, that the federal tax system is unconstitutional. Some of the speakers at these meetings were lawyers who purported to give professional opinions about the invalidity of the federal income tax laws. Cheek produced a letter from an attorney stating that the Sixteenth Amendment did not authorize a tax on wages and salaries, but only on gain or profit. Petitioner's defense was that, based on the indoctrination he received from this group and from his own study, he sincerely believed that the tax laws were being unconstitutionally enforced and that his actions during the 1980–1986 period were lawful. He therefore argued that he had acted without the willfulness required for conviction of the various offenses with which he was charged.

In the course of its instructions, the trial court advised the jury that, to prove "willfulness," the Government must prove the voluntary and intentional violation of a known legal duty, a burden that could not be proved by showing mistake, ignorance, or negligence. The court further advised the jury that an objectively reasonable good-faith misunderstanding of the law would negate willfulness, but mere disagreement with the law would not. . . .

The jury returned a verdict finding petitioner guilty on all counts.

Petitioner appealed his convictions, arguing that the District Court erred by instructing the jury that only an objectively reasonable misunderstanding of the law negates the statutory willfulness requirement. The United States Court of

Appeals for the Seventh Circuit rejected that contention, and affirmed the convictions. In prior cases, the Seventh Circuit had made clear that good-faith misunderstanding of the law negates willfulness only if the defendant's beliefs are objectively reasonable; in the Seventh Circuit, even actual ignorance is not a defense unless the defendant's ignorance was itself objectively reasonable. In its opinion in this case, the court noted that several specified beliefs, including the beliefs that the tax laws are unconstitutional and that wages are not income, would not be objectively reasonable. . . .

Tax Offenses Get Special Treatment

The general rule that ignorance of the law or a mistake of law is no defense to criminal prosecution is deeply rooted in the American legal system. Based on the notion that the law is definite and knowable, the common law presumed that every person knew the law. This common law rule has been applied by the Court in numerous cases construing criminal statutes.

The proliferation of statutes and regulations has sometimes made it difficult for the average citizen to know and comprehend the extent of the duties and obligations imposed by the tax laws. Congress has accordingly softened the impact of the common law presumption by making specific intent to violate the law an element of certain federal criminal tax offenses. Thus, the Court almost 60 years ago interpreted the statutory term "willfully" as used in the federal criminal tax statutes as carving out an exception to the traditional rule. This special treatment of criminal tax offenses is largely due to the complexity of the tax laws. . . .

Willfulness, as construed by our prior decisions in criminal tax cases, requires the Government to prove that the law imposed a duty on the defendant, that the defendant knew of this duty, and that he voluntarily and intentionally violated that duty. We deal first with the case where the issue is whether the defendant knew of the duty purportedly imposed by the provision of the statute or regulation he is accused of violating, a case in which there is no claim that the provision at issue is invalid. In such a case, if the Government proves actual knowledge of the pertinent legal duty, the prosecution, without more, has satisfied the knowledge component of the willfulness requirement. But carrying this burden requires negating a defendant's claim of ignorance of the law or a claim that, because of a misunderstanding of the law, he had a good-faith belief that he was not violating any of the provisions of the tax laws. This is so because one cannot be aware that the law imposes a duty upon him and yet be ignorant of it, misunderstand the law, or believe that the duty does not exist. In the end, the issue is whether, based on all the evidence, the Government has proved that the defendant was aware of the duty at issue, which cannot be true if the jury credits a good-faith misunderstanding and belief submission, whether or not the claimed belief or misunderstanding is objectively reasonable.

In this case, if Cheek asserted that he truly believed that the Internal Revenue Code did not purport to treat wages as income, and the jury believed him, the Government would not have carried its burden to prove willfulness, however unreasonable a court might deem such a belief. Of course, in deciding whether to credit Cheek's good-faith belief claim, the jury would be free to consider any admissible evidence from any source showing that Cheek was aware of his duty to file a return and to treat wages as income. . . .

We thus disagree with the Court of Appeals' requirement that a claimed good-faith belief must be objectively reasonable if it is to be considered as possibly negating the Government's evidence purporting to show a defendant's awareness of the legal duty at issue. Knowledge and belief are characteristically questions for the factfinder, in this case the jury. Characterizing a particular belief as not objectively reasonable transforms the inquiry into a legal one, and would prevent the jury from considering it. It would of course be proper to exclude evidence having no relevance or probative value with respect to willfulness, but it is not contrary to common sense, let alone impossible, for a defendant to be ignorant of his duty based on an irrational belief that he has no duty, and forbidding the jury to consider evidence that might negate willfulness would raise a serious question under the Sixth Amendment's jury trial provision. . . .

It was therefore error to instruct the jury to disregard evidence of Cheek's understanding that, within the meaning of the tax laws, he was not a person required to file a return or to pay income taxes and that wages are not taxable income, as incredible as such misunderstandings of and beliefs about the law might be. Of course, the more unreasonable the asserted beliefs or misunderstandings are, the more likely the jury will consider them to be nothing more than simple disagreement with known legal duties imposed by the tax laws, and will find that the Government has carried its burden of proving knowledge.

Ignorance of the Law

Cheek asserted in the trial court that he should be acquitted because he believed in good faith that the income tax law is unconstitutional as applied to him, and thus could not legally impose any duty upon him of which he should have been aware. Such a submission is unsound, not because Cheek's constitutional arguments are not objectively reasonable or frivolous, which they surely are, but because . . . claims that some of the provisions of the tax code are unconstitutional are submissions of a different order. They do not arise from innocent mistakes caused by the complexity of the Internal Revenue Code. Rather, they reveal full knowledge of the provisions at issue and a studied conclusion, however wrong, that those provisions are invalid and unenforceable.

Thus, in this case, Cheek paid his taxes for years, but after attending various seminars and based on his own study, he concluded that the income tax laws could not constitutionally require him to pay a tax.

We do not believe that Congress contemplated that such a taxpayer, without risking criminal prosecution, could ignore the duties imposed upon him by the Internal Revenue Code and refuse to utilize the mechanisms provided by Congress to present his claims of invalidity to the courts and to abide by their decisions. There is no doubt that Cheek, from year to year, was free to pay the tax that the law purported to require, file for a refund and, if denied, present his claims of invalidity, constitutional or otherwise, to the courts. . . .

We thus hold that, in a case like this, a defendant's views about the validity of the tax statutes are irrelevant to the issue of willfulness, need not be heard by the jury, and if they are, an instruction to disregard them would be proper. For this purpose, it makes no difference whether the claims of invalidity are frivolous or have substance. It was therefore not error in this case for the District Judge to instruct the jury not to consider Cheek's claims that the tax laws were unconstitutional. However, it was error for the court to instruct the jury that petitioner's asserted beliefs that wages are not income and that he was not a taxpayer within the meaning of the Internal Revenue Code should not be considered by the jury in determining whether Cheek had acted willfully.

For the reasons set forth in the opinion above, the judgment of the Court of Appeals is vacated, and the case is remanded for further proceedings consistent with this opinion.

*"The Court's opinion today ... will en-
courage taxpayers to cling to frivolous
views of the law in the hope of convincing a jury of their sincerity."*

Dissenting Opinion:
The Court's Opinion
Will Encourage Frivolous
Views of the Tax Law

Harry S. Blackmun

*Harry S. Blackmun was a justice of the Supreme Court from
1970 to 1994. He is best known as the author of the majority
opinion in* Roe v. Wade, *the decision that overturned laws re-
stricting abortion. In his following brief dissent in* Cheek v.
United States, *he states that it is incomprehensible to him how
any taxpayer of competent mentality can believe that his wages
are not income, especially this particular taxpayer, who was intelligent enough to be a licensed pilot for a major airline. Blackmun declares that he fears the Court's decision "will encourage
taxpayers to cling to frivolous views of the law in the hope of
convincing a jury of their sincerity."*

It seems to me that we are concerned in this case not with
"the complexity of the tax laws," but with the income tax
law in its most elementary and basic aspect: Is a wage earner a
taxpayer and are wages income?

The Court acknowledges that the conclusively established
standard for willfulness under the applicable statutes is the

Harry S. Blackmun, dissenting opinion, *Cheek v. United States*, U.S. Supreme Court,
January 8, 1991. Reproduced by permission.

"voluntary, intentional violation of a known legal duty." That being so, it is incomprehensible to me how, in this day, more than 70 years after the institution of our present federal income tax system with the passage of the Revenue Act of 1913, any taxpayer of competent mentality can assert as his defense to charges of statutory willfulness the proposition that the wage he receives for his labor is not income, irrespective of a cult that says otherwise and advises the gullible to resist income tax collections. One might note in passing that this particular taxpayer, after all, was a licensed pilot for one of our major commercial airlines; he presumably was a person of at least minimum intellectual competence.

The District Court's instruction that an objectively reasonable and good-faith misunderstanding of the law negates willfulness lends further, rather than less, protection to this defendant, for it added an additional hurdle for the prosecution to overcome. Petitioner should be grateful for this further protection, rather than be opposed to it.

This Court's opinion today, I fear, will encourage taxpayers to cling to frivolous views of the law in the hope of convincing a jury of their sincerity. If that ensues, I suspect we have gone beyond the limits of common sense.

While I may not agree with every word the Court of Appeals has enunciated in its opinion, I would affirm its judgment in this case. I therefore dissent.

> "It was therefore error for the trial judge to instruct the jury to disregard evidence of Cheek's understanding that ... he was not a person required to file a return or to pay income taxes and that wages are not taxable income, as incredible as such misunderstandings of and beliefs about the law might be."
>
> Cheek v. U.S., Supreme Court (1991)

The Court's Ruling Does Not Support the Tax Protest Movement

James Lanting

James Lanting is a practicing attorney. In the following article he explains the tax protest movement, which is a group of Americans who refuse to pay income taxes because they claim tax laws are invalid and unconstitutional. Some of them have been convicted of not only tax evasion but also fraud, and Lanting notes that unfortunately some innocent people have been taken in by them. The Supreme Court ruled in Cheek v. United States *that a genuine belief that no taxes are owed need not be reasonable, but mere disagreement with the tax law is not a defense, so the ruling will not help tax protestors who are aware of that law's requirements. Furthermore, even honest nonpayers face the expense and burden of a trial.*

James Lanting, "U.S. Supreme Court Overturns Tax Protester's Convictions," *Standard Bearer*, April 1, 1991. Reproduced by permission.

The tax protest movement is a loosely organized group of Americans who refuse to file income tax returns and pay income tax. Leaders of the movement conduct seminars and distribute tapes, books, and "legal opinions" contending that the U.S. tax laws are invalid and unconstitutional. In the last decade, many of the movement's leaders themselves have been convicted of tax evasion, conspiracy, and fraud, chiefly due to their failure to report the prodigious income generated from their lucrative seminars and publications.

Some evangelical Christians, understandably distressed by the government's perennial squandering and abuse of our tax dollars, have been persuaded by these charlatans to entertain the notion that federal income taxes are voluntary. Tragically enough, many of them are now languishing in federal penitentiaries and are insolvent following the government's seizure of their bank accounts and real estate to satisfy their delinquent taxes, accumulated interest, and heavy penalties.

Cheek Convicted by Jury

A 47-year old veteran airline pilot, described by his lawyer as a "gullible victim of the tax protest movement," recently had his tax evasion conviction overturned by the U.S. Supreme Court. John Cheek joined the tax protest movement in the late '70s and refused to file tax returns or pay taxes on his pilot's wages from 1980–1983. Moreover, by the mid-1980s, he was claiming over 60 exemptions on his W-4 forms.

Federal law provides that any person who "*willfully* attempts in any manner to evade or defeat any tax" is guilty of a felony. Mr. Cheek was indicted and tried on three counts of willfully attempting to evade his income taxes.

Although Cheek admitted at trial that he did not file returns or pay any tax for the years in question, his defense was that his actions were not "willful" evasion. Cheek testified that he was indoctrinated at tax protest seminars and consequently sincerely (albeit mistakenly) believed that (1) his wages were not "income" and that he was not a "taxpayer" within the meaning of the tax laws; and (2) that the tax laws were unconstitutional. He therefore argued that he acted without the willfulness required for conviction.

The trial judge ruled that these unusual beliefs were not "objectively reasonable" and essentially instructed the jury to ignore these purported defenses. After lengthy deliberations, the jury convicted Cheek on all counts. He was sentenced to one year in jail and five years probation.

Misunderstanding Negates Willfulness

Cheek appealed his conviction, arguing that it was error for the trial court to instruct the jury to disregard his admittedly mistaken beliefs about the tax laws just because they were not, in the judge's opinion, "objectively reasonable."

The U.S. Supreme Court, confronting its first tax protester case, partially agreed with Cheek and remanded his case for a new trial. The Court held that the trial judge erred in condemning as unreasonable Cheek's mistaken belief that he was not a "taxpayer" and that his pilot's wages were not "income." The Court ruled that it should have been a jury determination whether or not these beliefs were good-faith misunderstandings of his duty to pay taxes. In other words, the Court held that it was the jury's function, not the judge's, to decide whether these beliefs negated the requisite criminal intent.

Unconstitutionality No Defense

However, in a second part of its opinion, the Court unequivocally stated that his belief in the *unconstitutionality* of the tax laws is not a defense. Should Cheek have thought the tax laws unconstitutional, said the Court, he should have paid the tax and then filed for a refund. In that legal way, he could have challenged the constitutionality of the tax laws. Thus the Court held that a defendant's belief in the invalidity or unconstitutionality of the tax laws is irrelevant and inadmissible, since it smacks of mere *disagreement* with the laws—which is never a defense.

Accordingly, the Court remanded the case for a retrial, instructing the judge to exclude Cheek's unconstitutionality defense but to permit a jury to determine whether Cheek's unusual notions regarding the definition of "income" and "taxpayer" were sincerely-held misunderstandings which may have negated his criminal intent. "Of course," said the Court, "the more unreasonable the asserted beliefs or misunderstandings are, the more likely the jury will consider them to be nothing more than disagreement with known legal duties."

A Caveat

Although the tax protest movement will undoubtedly consider the *Cheek* opinion to be a favorable ruling, a careful reading reveals otherwise, for several reasons.

First, the *Cheek* decision is very limited; it merely held that jury may consider the defense that a sincerely held misunderstanding of the tax laws negates criminal intent. That is not to say that any jury anywhere is going to "buy" such a defense. The Supreme Court itself ventured an opinion that such a defense appears to be "incredible."

Secondly, the Court clearly held that a defendant's belief in the invalidity or unconstitutionality of the tax laws is simply *disagreement*, not a *misunderstanding* of the laws. Under the *Cheek* decision, disagreement with the tax laws or a belief they are unconstitutional is *not* a defense. By far the majority of tax protesters do not misunderstand the tax laws, they simply disagree with them. Such a purported defense is now clearly illegal and improper.

Thirdly, Cheek has not yet won his case; it was merely remanded for a new trial. Cheek now faces the expense, risk, and burden of a re-trial and perhaps even years of appeals or incarceration if he is convicted again.

Fourth, although a good-faith misunderstanding may be a defense to *criminal* charges, the *Cheek* decision in no way shields one from *civil* liability for all back taxes plus interest and onerous penalties. (In Cheek's case, he eventually paid over $150,000 in delinquent taxes, interest, and penalties in addition to $40,000 for attorney's fees during his years of appeal.)

Finally, Cheek prevailed on appeal only because his attorney argued that Cheek had been victimized and indoctrinated by unscrupulous tax protest leaders who had duped him into believing the mistaken notion that his wages were not "income." The *Cheek* decision can hardly be championed now by tax protest leaders.

Justice Blackmun, in his dissent, voiced some realistic warnings about the *Cheek* decision:

> It is incomprehensible to me how, in this day . . . any taxpayer of competent mentality can assert as his defense to statutory willfulness the proposition that the wage he receives for his labor is not income, irrespective of the cult that says otherwise and advises the gullible to resist income tax collections. The Court's opinion today. I fear, will encourage taxpayers to cling to frivolous views of the law in the hope of convincing a jury of their sincerity.

Accordingly, Reformed Christians must again be reminded that our Supreme Court still considers income tax payment a legal duty of all citizens and a willful evasion to be a felony in our land. And perhaps even more seriously, such unlawful activity consequently is also a violation of God's Word which comands us to obey our magistrates and unconditionally to render "taxes to whom taxes are due" (Rom 13:7; I Pet. 2:13; Matt. 22:21: Belgic Confession, Art. 36).

"If you truly believe that you don't owe taxes, you might not end up in jail, *but the IRS will still be able to come after you for the amounts you owe."*

The Court's Ruling Will Not Prevent Tax Evaders from Being Convicted

Jonathan R. Siegel

Jonathan R. Siegel is a professor of law at the George Washington University Law School. In the following article from his Web site about tax myths, he explains that it is true that it is not a crime for someone not to pay income tax if he or she truly believes he does not have to. However, he warns, there is still an obligation to pay later, with interest and penalties added. Ignorance of the law merely means the person cannot be convicted of crime, not that he or she does not owe taxes. Furthermore, he or she must convince a jury that this belief was genuine, and that it was not based on mere disagreement with the law. So tax protestors are putting themselves at considerable risk if they think pretending not to have known their taxes were due will keep them out of trouble.

"*I*t's not a crime not to pay income taxes, so long as you truly believe *you don't have to."*

Well, actually, this one turns out to be true. In the aptly-named case of *Cheek v. United States* (1991), the Supreme Court noted that the statute making it a crime to fail to pay

Jonathan R. Siegel, "It's Not a Crime Not to Pay Income Taxes, So Long as You *Truly Believe* You Don't Have To," Jon Siegel's Income Tax Protestors Page, January 31, 2007. Reproduced by permission of the author.

federal income taxes provides that the crime is committed only by someone who "willfully" fails to pay. The Supreme Court held that someone who truly believes that the law does not require him to pay taxes has not committed the crime of willfully failing to pay, even though his belief is wrong.

So you might think that the whole thing is simple—just *believe* that you don't have to pay any taxes, and—voila!—you don't. But be warned! Here are some details:

You Still Have to Pay

First of all, the belief that you don't have to pay taxes does not relieve you of your obligation to pay. At most, it means that failure to pay will not be a *crime*. If you owe taxes, you owe them, regardless of any erroneous beliefs you may have. So if you truly believe that you don't owe taxes, you might not end up in *jail*, but the IRS will still be able to come after you for the amounts you owe, and they can add on interest and civil penalties, which can add a considerable sum to your tax bill. There is, for example, a penalty of 20% for substantially understating the tax that you owe—and it can be 75% if the understatement is due to fraud. Moreover, lately, the courts have started tacking on their own penalties for making frivolous arguments about not owing taxes. Some courts routinely sock tax protestors for an extra $2000 or more for taking a frivolous appeal from IRS rulings. So your beliefs can end up being very expensive. (2009 update: Some courts have recently been imposing sanctions of $8000 for frivolous tax protestor arguments.)

Second, the Supreme Court placed some limits on the sources of permissible good faith beliefs that one doesn't owe taxes. The Court held that it is not a defense to a charge of willfully failing to file that one believed the income tax laws were unconstitutional. So if the reason you think you don't owe taxes is that you believe the tax laws are unconstitutional, that's not a defense.

The Jury Must Decide

Finally, and perhaps most important, if you get criminally prosecuted, your mere statement that you truly believed that you didn't owe any taxes is not automatically believed. It will be up to you to convince the jury of what your beliefs were, and it will be up to the jury to make the ultimate determination of whether you did or did not truly believe that you didn't owe any taxes. After all, you could be lying. You might know very well that you owe taxes, but be lying strategically in an effort to avoid prison. Since your inner beliefs are not subject to conclusive demonstration, it will be up to the jury to figure out what you really believed.

So a lot will depend on what type of jury you get. Perhaps you're hoping that you'll get a jury of tax skeptics, or just a foolish jury that you can try to persuade. Well, you might. Every now and then a tax protestor type manages to convince a jury that he really believed all this guff about not owing taxes, and the jury acquits. But you could also end up with a sensible jury, which can see through self-interested lies about a person's beliefs. You might also get an angry jury, made up of citizens who pay their taxes regularly and responsibly, and who don't have any patience with absurd arguments about how no one owes taxes.

Also, the judge will be giving the jury some instructions about how it should determine what your beliefs really are. One instruction that some judges give is that the more far-fetched an alleged belief is, the less likely it is that someone really believes it. So if the jury recognizes that the claim that no one owes taxes is absurd, which it is, the jury may be more ready to infer that the defendant is lying when he claims to believe it. The jury may be more ready to conclude that the defendant knew perfectly well that he owed taxes, and was only adopting a pretense of believing that he didn't, in an effort to avoid paying.

Another instruction that some judges give is that the requirement of willfulness exists to protect taxpayers who make innocent mistakes caused by the complexity of the tax code. This instruction, which has been upheld by the federal courts of appeals, might suggest to the jury that it is inappropriate to find a lack of willfulness for a defendant who holds typical tax protestor beliefs.

So while it is true that a genuine belief that you don't owe taxes means that failure to pay is not a crime, and while it is true that a tax protestor gets acquitted on this ground every now and again, if you adopt this strategy, you're putting your freedom at considerable risk. You're banking on what some jury is likely to conclude about your beliefs. If the jury finds that you believed you owed taxes and deliberately did not pay, you'll be heading for jail.

> *"The message to would-be tax evaders is clear: If you don't know anything about taxes, you can't be guilty of tax crime. Don't learn, because knowledge can only be used against you."*

The Tax Loophole Provided by *Cheek* Should Be Closed

Mark C. Winings

Mark C. Winings is an attorney whose practice focuses on banking, finance, real estate, and corporate law. In the following article he argues that the law should require a taxpayer's mistaken belief that he does not owe taxes to be objectively reasonable, in addition to being honestly held, in order to be a defense against criminal charges. According to the Supreme Court's ruling in Cheek v. United States, *prosecutors must prove that a defendant knew he was breaking the tax law, and even unreasonable beliefs about the law can qualify as evidence that he did not. This is not fair, Winings says, because it does not apply to other white-collar crimes. Moreover, it discourages people from learning about tax laws. In his opinion, ignorance should not be rewarded.*

Comedian Steve Martin, in an old stand-up routine, tells his audience that by following his simple plan, they can have a million dollars and never pay taxes. Step one, he advises, is to get a million dollars. Step two, naturally, is to not pay taxes. The beauty of the strategy, however, rests in step

Mark C. Winings, "Ignorance Is Bliss, Especially for the Tax Evader," *Journal of Criminal Law and Criminology*, Fall 1993, pp. 575–603. Copyright © 1993 by Northwestern University, School of Law. Reproduced by permission.

three. When the Internal Revenue Service agent comes to your door asking why you have not paid taxes, Martin says, simply smile and say, "I forgot."

Although Martin was joking, under current Federal tax law, his plan succeeds. "Forgetting" to pay your taxes actually constitutes a valid defense to a charge of criminal tax evasion. Other defenses include believing that wages are not income or that paper currency is not money. Forget what your criminal law professor taught you. Ignorance of the law is an excuse in tax crimes, and the only joke is on the Internal Revenue Service.

The Internal Revenue Service (IRS) may assess criminal charges on taxpayers who willfully evade the payment of income taxes. In *Cheek v. United States*, the United States Supreme Court interpreted "willfully" as the taxpayer's actual knowledge that his actions violate the law. One who avoids taxes can avoid conviction by demonstrating his truly held belief that he owes no taxes. Moreover, the jury may not consider the reasonableness of this belief.

The Supreme Court's interpretation of "willfulness" in *Cheek* created a huge tax loophole. This comment argues that Congress must close the *Cheek* loophole by modifying the Internal Revenue Code. The law should hold a taxpayer in "willful" violation of the tax code if he either subjectively intends to break the law or if, under an objective standard, he unreasonably relies upon a mistaken belief about the tax law. . . .

"Willfulness" in Tax Law

The Internal Revenue Code uses the word "willful" liberally. Before the Court addressed the issue in *Cheek v. United States*, several circuit courts formulated their own interpretations of the willfulness component of tax crime.

The Fifth and Tenth Circuits applied a subjective test, which asked whether a tax crime defendant truly believed his actions complied with the law. In *United States v. Phillips*, a taxpayer defended himself on the grounds that he truly believed his wages were not income. The trial court had instructed the jury as follows:

> A mistake of law must be objectively reasonable to be a defense. If you find that the defendant did not have a reasonable ground for his belief, then regardless of the defendant's sincerity of belief, you may find that he did not have a good faith misunderstanding of the requirements of the law.

The trial court convicted the defendant under this instruction, but the Tenth Circuit reversed and remanded for a new trial. The court reasoned that by requiring a "willful" violation, Congress did not intend to impose criminal liability on those who rely on their good faith belief that they need not file a tax return. For this reason, the Tenth Circuit stated, courts should use a subjective standard when evaluating a defendant's claim that he did not know he was breaking the law. Thus, prosecutors must prove that tax evasion defendants subjectively intended to disobey the law.

The subjective intent standard of *Phillips* paralleled decisions in several other circuits. The circuits following the subjective standard have carefully distinguished between those taxpayers who misunderstand the law and those who understand but disagree with it. A taxpayer who is unaware of the law may assert ignorance as a defense, but a taxpayer who merely disagrees with the law may not.

Before the Supreme Court decided *Cheek*, the Seventh Circuit took a different approach by permitting only honest and reasonable mistakes as a defense to a tax evasion charge. The Seventh Circuit applied an objective test to the taxpayer's mistaken "belief." If a reasonable person would realize the groundlessness of the belief, the court may impose criminal sanctions. A defendant's honest but unreasonable belief that he owed no taxes was held to be no defense to tax evasion. If a court found the defendant's belief unreasonable as a matter of law, the sincerity of the belief became irrelevant. In such a case, the court was not obligated to accept evidence demonstrating that the defendant actually held the mistaken belief. . . .

The *Cheek* Decision

In 1991, the United States Supreme Court addressed the conflict between the circuits in *Cheek v. United States*. In *Cheek*, the Court faced the task of defining "willfully," and determining whether a defendant taxpayer could use an honest but unreasonable mistake of law as a defense. . . .

The Supreme Court began by noting the traditional principle that ignorance of the law provides no defense and the corresponding presumption that every person knows the law because the law is "definite and knowable." The Court said, however, that the growing volume and complexity of statutes and regulations, including the Internal Revenue Code, raised questions about the soundness of this premise. Consequently, the Court long ago determined that Congress used the word "willfully" in the tax code to carve an exception to the traditional principle. The Court recalled its sixty year old statement from *United States v. Murdock*:

> Congress did not intend that a person, by reason of a bona fide misunderstanding as to his liability for the tax, as to his duty to make a return, or as to the adequacy of the records he maintained, should become a criminal by his mere failure to measure up to the prescribed standard of conduct.

Since *Murdock*, the Court had defined "willfully," in the context of the tax code, as a "voluntary, intentional violation of a known legal duty."

Cheek argued that by allowing the jury to consider the objective reasonableness of his beliefs, the district court's instruction was inconsistent with the *Murdock* interpretation. The Supreme Court agreed, stating that the jury should have determined whether the prosecution had proved Cheek's awareness of his duty to file return and pay taxes. The objective reasonableness of his claimed belief or misunderstanding was completely irrelevant to this question. No matter how unreasonable a jury might find Cheek's belief that the Internal Revenue Code did not treat wages as income, if they found that Cheek truly held such a belief, they must acquit him.

The Court rejected Cheek's claim that he believed income tax laws violated the Constitution. This belief, said the Court, was not an innocently mistaken belief about the content of the law, but a studied conclusion that the law was invalid. In other words, Cheek did not make a mistake about the law; he simply disagreed with it.

Over the dissent of Justices [Harry S.] Blackmun and [Thurgood] Marshall, who feared that the majority opinion would "encourage taxpayers to cling to frivolous views . . . in the hope of convincing a jury of their sincerity," the Court vacated and remanded the case. The Seventh Circuit, the majority held, erred by allowing objective reasonableness to enter the calculation. Thus, *Cheek* demands a purely subjective inquiry into the taxpayer's mental state to determine whether the defendant willfully violated the tax code.

"Willfulness" After *Cheek*

Commentators have given *Cheek* mixed reviews. One commentator [Dwight W. Stone] hails the decision for striking "a sensible balance between disciplined regard for the dictates of precedent and awareness of practical policy ramifications." The Seventh Circuit approach, he argues, would have "benefitted judicial economy at the expense of logic and consistency." Another commentator [Walter T. Henderson] however, contends that the Supreme Court's narrow interpretation of "willfulness" emasculates the Internal Revenue Code by making it virtually impossible to convict tax evaders.

Cheek has raised new questions as the circuits struggle to determine the scope of Cheek's definition of "willfulness." Circuit courts have construed *Cheek* narrowly in some cases but broadly in others. . . .

In *United States v. Donovan*, the government charged a bank president with willfully failing to file currency transaction reports, which the law requires whenever a bank accepts any cash deposit exceeding $10,000. The defendant argued that *Cheek* established a purely subjective test for every white collar crime which includes willfulness as an element of the offense. Consequently, he asked for a *Cheek* jury instruction which would require the jury to exonerate him if they found that he honestly did not know that his failure to report the transaction violated the currency transaction report filing requirement, regardless of the reasonableness of his belief.

Rejecting the defendant's argument, the court explicitly stated that *Cheek* applies only to tax crimes. . . .

Thus, as subsequent non-tax decisions make clear, *Cheek* created a specific, narrow exception to the traditional common law principle that ignorance is no defense. Ignorance of the law is still no defense—unless the crime is tax evasion. . . .

The Need for an Objective Standard

Although the Supreme Court has clearly defined willfulness, this definition is not necessarily optimal in terms of benefits to society and fairness to individual taxpayers. . . . This comment argues that the Seventh Circuit's pre-*Cheek* approach is superior to the present state of the law. Before a defendant should be permitted to claim mistake or ignorance as a defense, the law should require her to demonstrate that her mistaken belief or lack of knowledge was objectively reasonable. An unreasonable belief, even if sincerely held, should not serve as a defense to tax evasion.

Under this proposal, a taxpayer's mistaken belief would excuse the taxpayer from criminal liability only if the belief is both objectively reasonable and sincerely held. Similar to a negligence standard, the law would presume the taxpayer to have at least a minimal knowledge of the tax law. This standard would not require taxpayer expertise or even familiarity with all aspects of tax law. It simply presumes that all Americans are aware that taxes exist and insists they take basic steps to learn the fundamentals, such as reading the IRS tax form instructions.

Using an objective reasonableness standard would bring tax law into alignment with other areas of criminal law. Also, an objective standard is fair to the defendant, it better prevents flagrant abuse of the tax system, and it would improve tax compliance. Congressional action, in the form of either replacing or redefining the word "willfully" in the Internal Revenue Code, could effectively realize the advantages that an objective approach would generate without upsetting a long line of Supreme Court jurisprudence. . . .

The criminal law currently applies the subjective standard only in tax cases, even though the special treatment of tax defendants has no logical foundation. The disparate treatment of tax crime defendants and other white collar crime defendants is unfair because it is based on transparent distinctions. Using an objective standard in both instances would make the law more consistent, and therefore more just.

Objective Standard Provides Fairness

John Cheek's Seventh Circuit brief analogizes his indoctrination into a tax protest group to the foibles of a naive fraud victim who is taken in by a smooth-talking "con man." Cheek compares the tax protestors who persuaded him that their beliefs were true to "snake-oil salesmen of lore" and argues that he "bought their desert real estate and their wellness potions." Unlike the sucker who buys snake-oil, however, John Cheek and the others directly benefitted from being "taken in." Because he benefitted, the law need not sympathize with him as though he were a victim. Cheek and other tax protestors more closely resemble a person who buys a new color television set from the back of a truck in an alley for twenty dollars. Despite suspicions about the legitimacy of the sale and the television's origin, the purchaser keeps the television and remains silent. . . .

An objective standard would impose a duty on taxpayers to know the fundamental concepts of the tax law. It would not require the taxpayer to understand all the nuances of the tax code. The law would simply presume that all citizens know that a tax system exists which requires taxpayers to pay income taxes, just as it presumes that everyone who drives a car knows the traffic laws. . . .

Objective Standard Prevents Abuse

One of the most compelling reasons to move away from the subjective standard of *Cheek* . . . is to enable effective prosecution of those who do not "truly" hold their mistaken beliefs— those who either consciously cheat on their taxes or intentionally avoid learning the applicable rules and then feign ignorance when caught. Most taxpayers do not realize that the "ignorance of the law is no excuse" maxim does not apply to tax law. As a result, the ignorance defense is most often invoked by sly taxpayers who are well aware of the heavy burden the government bears in tax crime prosecution.

The objective standard would add another hurdle for manipulative taxpayers to clear before the law exonerates them. The Seventh Circuit used the objective approach, in large part, for this reason. The *Cheek* decision, in overruling the Seventh Circuit, invites abuse.

Allowing ignorance as a defense without regard to reasonableness creates undesirable incentives. The law encourages taxpayer ignorance, because the prosecution can use a taxpayer's knowledge against him. . . .

The objective standard, on the other hand, provides an incentive for the taxpayer to learn. To escape criminal liability, the taxpayer need not hold completely accurate beliefs, but she must hold reasonable beliefs. A taxpayer who generally familiarizes herself with the tax rules, understands her obligation to file a return, and makes an honest attempt to comply should have little difficulty meeting this standard. . . .

The subjective standard also encourages defendants to lie to the jury. Since the case focuses on the defendant's state of mind at the time of the alleged transgression, the defendant's personal testimony becomes extremely important. Although the subjective standard permits the jury to consider objective factors, the jury must ultimately determine what the taxpayer actually believed. Because corroborating evidence on this question is understandably hard to produce, the jury might not demand any, and instead place great weight on the defendant's explanation. A skillful liar thus has a better chance of acquittal in a tax case than in non-tax criminal cases, where the prosecution has greater opportunity to present evidence contradicting the defendant's testimony.

The nature of tax crime especially tempts a defendant to lie, not only because it is in the offender's best interest and is likely to work, but because, in the offender's mind, it is easy to justify from a moral standpoint. Tax evaders often rationalize non-compliance on the grounds that the government wastes tax dollars anyway, that loopholes unfairly allow others to avoid taxes, or that failure to comply does not really hurt anyone. Ordinarily law-abiding citizens, whose personal moral codes would prevent them from committing other crimes or lying about it afterwards, might intentionally violate tax laws and then lie to a jury without even flinching. . . .

In addition to encouraging ignorance of the law and deception, the subjective standard encourages people to lie to themselves. If a taxpayer can convince herself that her view of the tax law, no matter how mistaken, is correct, she technically has not committed a crime. In many cases, this self-persuasion will not prove too difficult a task. Most taxpayers are probably all too eager to believe whatever interpretation will reduce their taxes the most. . . .

By some estimates, there are over 13,000 tax protestors in the United States. They call themselves "great American heroes," and they conduct seminars to teach their followers, among other things, that the Sixteenth Amendment is unconstitutional. They instruct followers to claim hundreds of dependents on their W-4s, thereby preventing income from being withheld and to file frivolous tax returns. They encourage followers to obtain a jury trial so that sympathetic jury members will acquit after the jurors themselves are indoctrinated into the tax protest movement during the course of the trial. True "tax protestors" are not really ignorant of the law; they simply disagree with it. . . .

Tax protestors hold various beliefs about taxation, few of which are objectively reasonable. One defendant, for instance, said he failed to pay taxes because he believed that IRS agents were "Satan's little helpers." Whatever their belief, tax protestors do not pay taxes and jam court dockets with frivolous litigation. Tax protestors drain judicial resources which could be better spent elsewhere. Tax dollars are lost at both ends: revenues lost because protestors do not pay taxes, and revenues spent bringing them to justice. . . .

The case of John L. Cheek illustrates the need for an objective standard. A sophisticated commercial airline pilot claims to believe that his wages are not income and that he has over fifty dependents. Were these beliefs objectively reasonable? Certainly not. Were they truly held? Given the fact that for most of his adult life, Cheek had properly filed his tax returns, it is hard to believe that he was genuinely unaware of his obligations. A more plausible explanation is that John Cheek was nothing more than a tax protestor who disagreed with the tax laws. . . .

Because revenue collection in a voluntary system depends so heavily on taxpayer cooperation, the law should not allow ignorance as a defense. An objective standard encourages taxpayers to learn and follow the law. If a taxpayer knows the IRS is watching and will press criminal charges unless he acts reasonably, he will be all the more inclined to look up the rule in question. Under a purely subjective standard, where ignorance is bliss, that same taxpayer may simply assume that the rule works in his favor. After all, what he does not know cannot hurt him. . . .

In *United States v. Cheek*, the Supreme Court made it clear that the traditional maxim "ignorance of the law is no defense" does not apply to tax crimes. A taxpayer may behave outrageously, even to the point of not paying any taxes, without criminal penalty, as long as the taxpayer subjectively believes he is obeying the law.

The message to would-be tax evaders is clear: If you don't know anything about taxes, you can't be guilty of tax crime. Don't learn, because knowledge can only be used against you. If an armed robbery defendant cried "I forgot armed robbery was illegal," society would scornfully convict him. Failing to convict in such a case would allow that individual's beliefs to trump the law itself. . . .

While some areas of the tax law are complicated, the fundamental concept is really quite simple: Those who earn income must pay taxes. The IRS, in fact, tries to simplify the tax laws and even provides free assistance to those who request it. The tax law is not complex enough to justify a departure from one of the oldest and most sensible principles of common law. Ignorance should not be rewarded; it should be punished. Ignorance should not be bliss; it should be perilous.

CHAPTER 3

States May Not Require Out-of-State Companies to Collect Sales Taxes

Case Overview

Quill v. North Dakota (1992)

In most states, a tax must be paid on purchases. This is called a sales tax although the tax is owed by the buyer, not the seller, and the seller is responsible for collecting it. Consumers who buy from out-of-state sellers owe an equivalent tax called a use tax, which in theory they compute and send to the state; but few people do this, or are even aware that they are supposed to. Many make purchases on the Internet specifically for the purpose of avoiding sales tax on them.

Because use tax laws are not enforced, state governments lose a great deal of tax revenue to which they believe they are entitled. They would like to make out-of-state sellers collect the tax. But merchants resist collecting taxes for states other than their own because it is expensive to do the paperwork, and also because charging sales tax might cause them to lose out-of-state customers. This has been a contentious issue for many years. In a well-known 1967 case, *National Bellas Hess v. Department of Revenue of the State of Illinois*, the Supreme Court ruled that sellers who did not have any "nexus" in a state—that is, any physical presence such as a store, warehouse, or salespeople—did not have to collect use tax from its residents. "If the power of Illinois to impose use tax burdens upon National were upheld, the resulting impediments upon the free conduct of its interstate business would be neither imaginary nor remote," said the Court. "For if Illinois can impose such burdens, so can every other State, and so, indeed, can every municipality, every school district, and every other political subdivision throughout the Nation with power to impose sales and use taxes. . . . The very purpose of the Commerce Clause [of the Constitution] was to ensure a national economy free from such unjustifiable local entanglements."

In 1992 the question again came before the Supreme Court in *Quill v. North Dakota.* North Dakota maintained that the mail-order office supply company Quill did have a nexus in the state because it sent frequent advertisements to customers there and owned the software they used for placing orders. The Supreme Court of North Dakota had "declined to follow *Bellas Hess* because 'the tremendous social, economic, commercial, and legal innovations' of the past quarter century have rendered its holding 'obsolete.'" So, said the U.S. Supreme Court, "We must either reverse the State Supreme Court or overrule *Bellas Hess.*"

Overruling its own earlier decision is a serious step for the Supreme Court to take, and it is not done without a strong reason. In this case the Court decided that because of intervening decisions, the due process clause of the Constitution no longer provided legal grounds for excusing merchants from collecting tax on out-of-state purchases, but that the commerce clause still did. The commerce clause, it said, is concerned with the effects of state regulation on the national economy. Having a specific criterion (in legal terms called a "bright line") for determining which retailers have to collect tax prevents undue burdens on interstate commerce, and therefore the Court let the physical presence requirement stand; however, it stated that this requirement could be changed by Congress.

In the years since *Quill,* the growth of commercial activity on the Internet has led to a dramatic rise in the number of interstate transactions. Accordingly, state governments have increasingly been pressuring Congress to pass a law requiring sellers to collect sales tax on all purchases. Retailers that have stores in many states also favor it because they do not think it is fair for Internet-only businesses to be given a competitive advantage. Most consumers, on the other hand, feel that Internet purchases should remain tax-free, whether or not they realize that they are supposed to be paying use taxes on those purchases anyway.

The issue has heated up since 2008, when the state of New York passed a law that closed what it considered a loophole in the *Quill* ruling. It created a tax commonly called the "Amazon Tax," after the major Internet retailer Amazon.com, declaring that Amazon did have a physical presence in New York because it had affiliates there. (Affliliates are people who get a commission from Amazon when people go to the site from links on their Web pages; some are companies, but many are simply individuals such as bloggers.) Other states have followed suit, and Amazon has reacted by terminating its relationship with its affiliates in those states, depriving some of them of needed income. The controversy over this situation continues to grow.

| *"It is not unlikely that the mail order industry's dramatic growth over the last quarter century is due in part to the ... exemption from state taxation."*

Majority Opinion: Out-of-State Companies Cannot Be Compelled to Collect Sales Tax

John Paul Stevens

John Paul Stevens was, as of his retirement on June 29, 2010, the oldest and longest-serving member (since 1975) then sitting on the Supreme Court and was generally considered to be the leader of its liberal faction. In his opinion for the Court in Quill v. North Dakota, *he points out that the Court's holding in the earlier case of* Bellas Hess v. Illinois *(1967) relied on both the due process clause of the Constitution and the commerce clause. The due process clause requires a definite link between a requirement to collect sales tax and services provided by the state, such as services used by a local store. That clause, Stevens notes, has recently been interpreted differently from the way it was seen at the time of* Bellas Hess *and it now is seen to be enough that* Quill *solicits business from North Dakota customers through advertising. However, he says, the physical presence rule still furthers the ends of the commerce clause, the aim of which is to*

John Paul Stevens, majority opinion, *Quill v. North Dakota*, U.S. Supreme Court, May 26, 1992. Reproduced by permission.

prevent undue burdens on interstate commerce. For this reason, and because precedents should not be overturned without strong reason, the Court has decided to uphold Bellas Hess *in the case of* Quill.

Quill is a Delaware corporation with offices and warehouses in Illinois, California, and Georgia. None of its employees work or reside in North Dakota and its ownership of tangible property in that State is either insignificant or nonexistent. Quill sells office equipment and supplies; it solicits business through catalogs and flyers, advertisements in national periodicals, and telephone calls. Its annual national sales exceed $200,000,000, of which almost $1,000,000 are made to about 3,000 customers in North Dakota. It is the sixth largest vendor of office supplies in the State. It delivers all of its merchandise to its North Dakota customers by mail or common carrier from out of state locations.

As a corollary to its sales tax, North Dakota imposes a use tax upon property purchased for storage, use or consumption within the State. North Dakota requires every "retailer maintaining a place of business in" the State to collect the tax from the consumer and remit it to the State. In 1987 North Dakota amended the statutory definition of the term "retailer" to include "every person who engages in regular or systematic solicitation of a consumer market in th[e] state." State regulations in turn define "regular or systematic solicitation" to mean three or more advertisements within a 12 month period. Thus, since 1987, mail order companies that engage in such solicitation have been subject to the tax even if they maintain no property or personnel in North Dakota.

Quill has taken the position that North Dakota does not have the power to compel it to collect a use tax from its North Dakota customers. Consequently, the State, through its Tax Commissioner, filed this action to require Quill to pay taxes (as well as interest and penalties) on all such sales made after

July 1, 1987. The trial court ruled in Quill's favor, finding the case indistinguishable from *Bellas Hess v. Illinois* [1967]; specifically, it found that because the State had not shown that it had spent tax revenues for the benefit of the mail order business, there was no "nexus [connection] to allow the state to define retailer in the manner it chose."

The North Dakota Supreme Court reversed, concluding that "wholesale changes" in both the economy and the law made it inappropriate to follow *Bellas Hess* today. The principal economic change noted by the court was the remarkable growth of the mail order business "from a relatively inconsequential market niche" in 1967 to a "goliath" with annual sales that reached "the staggering figure of $183.3 billion in 1989." Moreover, the court observed, advances in computer technology greatly eased the burden of compliance with a "'welter of complicated obligations'" imposed by state and local taxing authorities.

Equally important, in the court's view, were the changes in the "legal landscape." With respect to the Commerce Clause, the court emphasized that *Complete Auto Transit, Inc. v. Brady* (1977), rejected the line of cases holding that the direct taxation of interstate commerce was impermissible and adopted instead a "consistent and rational method of inquiry [that focused on] the practical effect of [the] challenged tax." . . .

Turning to the case at hand, the State Court emphasized that North Dakota had created "an economic climate that fosters demand for" Quill's products, maintained a legal infrastructure that protected that market, and disposed of 24 tons of catalogs and flyers mailed by Quill into the State every year. Based on these facts, the court concluded that Quill's "economic presence" in North Dakota depended on services and benefits provided by the State and therefore generated "a constitutionally sufficient nexus to justify imposition of the purely administrative duty of collecting and remitting the use tax."

Constitutional Basis of the Decision

As in a number of other cases involving the application of state taxing statutes to out of state sellers, our holding in *Bellas Hess* relied on both the Due Process Clause and the Commerce Clause. . . . The clauses pose distinct limits on the taxing powers of the States. Accordingly, while a State may, consistent with the Due Process Clause, have the authority to tax a particular taxpayer, imposition of the tax may nonetheless violate the Commerce Clause. . . .

The Due Process Clause "requires some definite link, some minimum connection, between a state and the person, property or transaction it seeks to tax," *Miller Bros. Co. v. Maryland* (1954), and that the "income attributed to the State for tax purposes must be rationally related to 'values connected with the taxing State.'" *Moorman Mfg. Co. v. Bair* (1978). Here, we are concerned primarily with the first of these requirements. Prior to *Bellas Hess*, we had held that that requirement was satisfied in a variety of circumstances involving use taxes. For example, the presence of sales personnel in the State, or the maintenance of local retail stores in the State, justified the exercise of that power because the seller's local activities were "plainly accorded the protection and services of the taxing State." *Bellas Hess*. . . . These cases all involved some sort of physical presence within the State, and in *Bellas Hess* the Court suggested that such presence was not only sufficient for jurisdiction under the Due Process Clause, but also necessary. . . .

Our due process jurisprudence has evolved substantially in the 25 years since *Bellas Hess*. . . .

To the extent that our decisions have indicated that the Due Process Clause requires physical presence in a State for the imposition of duty to collect a use tax, we overrule those holdings as superseded by developments in the law of due process.

In this case, there is no question that Quill has purposefully directed its activities at North Dakota residents, that the magnitude of those contacts are more than sufficient for due process purposes, and that the use tax is related to the benefits Quill receives from access to the State. We therefore agree with the North Dakota Supreme Court's conclusion that the Due Process Clause does not bar enforcement of that State's use tax against Quill.

Article I, Section 8, cl. 3 of the Constitution expressly authorizes Congress to "regulate Commerce with foreign Nations, and among the several States." . . . The Commerce Clause is more than an affirmative grant of power; it has a negative sweep as well. The clause, in Justice [Harlan] Stone's phrasing, "by its own force" prohibits certain state actions that interfere with interstate commerce. . . .

In *Leloup v. Port of Mobile* (1888), we declared that "no State has the right to lay a tax on interstate commerce in any form." We later narrowed that rule and distinguished between direct burdens on interstate commerce, which were prohibited, and indirect burdens, which generally were not. . . .

In *National Geographic Society v. California Bd. of Equalization* (1977), we affirmed the continuing vitality of *Bellas Hess'* "sharp distinction . . . between mail order sellers with [a physical presence in the taxing] State and those . . . who do no more than communicate with customers in the State by mail or common carrier as part of a general interstate business." We have continued to cite *Bellas Hess* with approval ever since. . . .

The State contends that the nexus requirements imposed by the Due Process and Commerce Clauses are equivalent and that if, as we concluded above, a mail order house that lacks a physical presence in the taxing State nonetheless satisfies the due process "minimum contacts" test, then that corporation also meets the Commerce Clause "substantial nexus" test. We disagree. Despite the similarity in phrasing, the nexus requirements of the Due Process and Commerce Clauses are not identical. The two standards are animated by different constitutional concerns and policies.

Due process centrally concerns the fundamental fairness of governmental activity. Thus, at the most general level, the due process nexus analysis requires that we ask whether an individual's connections with a State are substantial enough to legitimate the State's exercise of power over him. . . . In contrast, the Commerce Clause, and its nexus requirement, are informed not so much by concerns about fairness for the individual defendant as by structural concerns about the effects of state regulation on the national economy. . . . We have ruled that that Clause prohibits discrimination against interstate commerce, and bars state regulations that unduly burden interstate commerce. . . .

No Good Reason to Overturn

Although we agree with the State Court's assessment of the evolution of our cases, we do not share its conclusion that this evolution indicates that the Commerce Clause ruling of *Bellas Hess* is no longer good law.

First, as the State Court itself noted, all of these cases involved taxpayers who had a physical presence in the taxing State and therefore do not directly conflict with the rule of *Bellas Hess* or compel that it be overruled. Second, and more importantly, although our Commerce Clause jurisprudence now favors more flexible balancing analyses, we have never intimated a desire to reject all established "bright line" tests. Although we have not, in our review of other types of taxes, articulated the same physical presence requirement that *Bellas Hess* established for sales and use taxes, that silence does not imply repudiation of the *Bellas Hess* rule. . . .

The bright line rule of *Bellas Hess* furthers the ends of the dormant Commerce Clause. Undue burdens on interstate commerce may be avoided not only by a case by case evaluation of the actual burdens imposed by particular regulations or taxes, but also, in some situations, by the demarcation of a discrete realm of commercial activity that is free from interstate taxation. *Bellas Hess* followed the latter approach and created a safe harbor for vendors "whose only connection with customers in the [taxing] State is by common carrier or the United States mail." Under *Bellas Hess*, such vendors are free from state imposed duties to collect sales and use taxes.

Like other bright line tests, the *Bellas Hess* rule appears artificial at its edges: whether or not a State may compel a vendor to collect a sales or use tax may turn on the presence in the taxing State of a small sales force, plant, or office. This artificiality, however, is more than offset by the benefits of a clear rule. Such a rule firmly establishes the boundaries of legitimate state authority to impose a duty to collect sales and use taxes and reduces litigation concerning those taxes. This benefit is important, for as we have so frequently noted, our law in this area is something of a "quagmire". . . .

Moreover, a bright line rule in the area of sales and use taxes also encourages settled expectations and, in doing so, fosters investment by businesses and individuals. Indeed, it is not unlikely that the mail order industry's dramatic growth over the last quarter century is due in part to the bright line exemption from state taxation created in *Bellas Hess*. . . .

In sum, although in our cases subsequent to *Bellas Hess* and concerning other types of taxes we have not adopted a similar bright line, physical presence requirement, our reasoning in those cases does not compel that we now reject the rule that *Bellas Hess* established in the area of sales and use taxes. To the contrary, the continuing value of a bright line rule in this area and the doctrine and principles of *stare decisis* [that judges should not overturn precedents without a strong reason] indicate that the *Bellas Hess* rule remains good law. For these reasons, we disagree with the North Dakota Supreme Court's conclusion that the time has come to renounce the bright line test of *Bellas Hess*.

This aspect of our decision is made easier by the fact that the underlying issue is not only one that Congress may be better qualified to resolve, but also one that Congress has the ultimate power to resolve. No matter how we evaluate the burdens that use taxes impose on interstate commerce, Congress remains free to disagree with our conclusions. Indeed, in recent years Congress has considered legislation that would "overrule" the *Bellas Hess* rule. Its decision not to take action in this direction may, of course, have been dictated by respect for our holding in *Bellas Hess* that the Due Process Clause prohibits States from imposing such taxes, but today we have put that problem to rest. Accordingly, Congress is now free to decide whether, when, and to what extent the States may burden interstate mail order concerns with a duty to collect use taxes.

| "In today's economy, physical presence frequently has very little to do with a transaction a State might seek to tax."

Dissenting Opinion: Exemption of Out-of-State Companies from Sales Tax Collection Is No Longer Justified

Byron R. White

Byron R. White was a justice of the Supreme Court from 1962 to 1993. In his youth he had been famous as an NFL football player. In his dissenting opinion in Quill v. North Dakota, *he disagrees with the portion of the Court's opinion that upheld the precedent set by* Bellas Hess v. Illinois *(1967), which held that for a marketer to be required to collect sales tax on out-of-state sales it must have a physical presence in the purchaser's state. White argues that there is no longer any connection between physical presence and sales and that it is illogical that a business with one salesperson in a state must for that reason have to collect tax on all its mail order and phone sales. Furthermore, he says, it is unfair to provide a tax shelter for some businesses but not for their competitors.*

The majority goes to some lengths to justify the *Bellas Hess v. Illinois* physical presence requirement under our Commerce Clause jurisprudence. I am unpersuaded by its interpretation of our cases. In *Bellas Hess*, the majority placed great

Byron R. White, opinion dissenting in part, *Quill v. North Dakota*, U.S. Supreme Court, May 26, 1992. Reproduced by permission.

weight on the interstate quality of the mail order sales, stating that "it is difficult to conceive of commercial transactions more exclusively interstate in character than the mail order transactions here involved." As the majority correctly observes, the idea of prohibiting States from taxing "exclusively interstate" transactions had been an important part of our jurisprudence for many decades.... But though it recognizes that *Bellas Hess* was decided amidst an upheaval in our Commerce Clause jurisprudence, ... the majority draws entirely the wrong conclusion from this period of ferment.... What we disavowed in *Complete Auto Transit v. Brady* was not just the "formal distinction between 'direct' and 'indirect' taxes on interstate commerce," but also the whole notion underlying the *Bellas Hess* physical presence rule—that "interstate commerce is immune from state taxation." *Complete Auto....*

When the Court announced its four part synthesis in *Complete Auto*, the nexus [connection] requirement was definitely traceable to concerns grounded in the Due Process Clause, and not the Commerce Clause, as the Court's discussion of the doctrinal antecedents for its rule made clear. For the Court now to assert that our Commerce Clause jurisprudence supports a separate notion of nexus is without precedent or explanation.

Physical Presence No Longer Relevant

Even were there to be such an independent requirement under the Commerce Clause, there is no relationship between the physical presence/nexus rule the Court retains and Commerce Clause considerations that allegedly justify it. Perhaps long ago a seller's "physical presence" was a sufficient part of a trade to condition imposition of a tax on such presence. But in today's economy, physical presence frequently has very little to do with a transaction a State might seek to tax. Wire transfers of money involving billions of dollars occur every day; purchasers place orders with sellers by fax, phone, and computer linkup; sellers ship goods by air, road, and sea through sundry delivery services without leaving their place of business. It is certainly true that the days of the door to door salesperson are not gone. Nevertheless, an out of state direct marketer derives numerous commercial benefits from the State in which it does business. These advantages include laws establishing sound local banking institutions to support credit transactions; courts to insure collection of the purchase price from the seller's customers; means of waste disposal from garbage generated by mail order solicitations; and creation and enforcement of consumer protection laws, which protect buyers and sellers alike, the former by ensuring that they will have a ready means of protecting against fraud, and the latter by creating a climate of consumer confidence that inures to the benefit of reputable dealers in mail order transactions. To create, for the first time, a nexus requirement under the Commerce Clause independent of that established for due process purposes is one thing; to attempt to justify an anachronistic notion of physical presence in economic terms is quite another.

The illogic of retaining the physical presence requirement in these circumstances is palpable. Under the majority's analysis, and our decision in *National Geographic v. California Board of Equilization*, an out of state seller with one salesperson in a State would be subject to use tax collection burdens on its entire mail order sales even if those sales were unrelated to the salesperson's solicitation efforts. By contrast, an out of state seller in a neighboring State could be the dominant business in the putative taxing State, creating the greatest infrastructure burdens and undercutting the State's home companies by its comparative price advantage in selling products free of use taxes, and yet not have to collect such taxes if it lacks a physical presence in the taxing State. The majority clings to the physical presence rule not because of any logical relation to fairness or any economic rationale related to principles underlying the Commerce Clause, but simply out of the supposed convenience of having a bright line rule. I am less impressed by the convenience of such adherence than the unfairness it produces. Here, convenience should give way.

Unfair Tax Shelter

Also very questionable is the rationality of perpetuating a rule that creates an interstate tax shelter for one form of business—mail order sellers—but no countervailing advantage for its competitors. If the Commerce Clause was intended to put businesses on an even playing field, the majority's rule is hardly a way to achieve that goal. Indeed, arguably even under the majority's explanation for its "Commerce Clause nexus" requirement, the unfairness of its rule on retailers other than direct marketers should be taken into account. I would think that protectionist rules favoring a $180 billion a year industry might come within the scope of such "structural concerns."

The Court attempts to justify what it rightly acknowledges is an "artificial" rule in several ways. First, it asserts that the *Bellas Hess* principle "firmly establishes the boundaries of legitimate state taxing authority and reduces litigation concerning state taxation." It is very doubtful, however, that the Court's opinion can achieve its aims. Certainly our cases now demonstrate two "bright line" rules for mail order sellers to follow: under the physical presence requirement reaffirmed here they will not be subjected to use tax collection if they have no physical presence in the taxing State; under the *National Geographic* rule, mail order sellers will be subject to use tax collection if they have some presence in the taxing State even if that activity has no relation to the transaction being taxed. Between these narrow lines lies the issue of what constitutes the requisite "physical presence" to justify imposition of use tax collection responsibilities.

Instead of confronting this question head on, the majority offers only a cursory analysis of whether Quill's physical presence in North Dakota was sufficient to justify its use tax collection burdens, despite briefing on this point by the State. North Dakota contends that even should the Court reaffirm the *Bellas Hess* rule, Quill's physical presence in North Dakota was sufficient to justify application of its use tax collection law. Quill concedes it owns software sent to its North Dakota customers, but suggests that such property is insufficient to justify a finding of nexus. In my view, the question of Quill's actual physical presence is sufficiently close to cast doubt on the majority's confidence that it is propounding a truly "bright line" rule. Reasonable minds surely can, and will, differ over what showing is required to make out a "physical presence" adequate to justify imposing responsibilities for use tax collection. And given the estimated loss in revenue to States of more than $3.2 billion this year alone, it is a sure bet that the vagaries of "physical presence" will be tested to their fullest in our courts. . . .

The Court's seeming but inadequate justification of encouraging settled expectations in fact connotes a substantive economic decision to favor out of state direct marketers to the detriment of other retailers. By justifying the *Bellas Hess* rule in terms of "the mail order industry's dramatic growth over the last quarter century," the Court is effectively imposing its own economic preferences in deciding this case. The Court's invitation to Congress to legislate in this area signals that its preferences are not immutable, but its approach is different from past instances in which we have deferred to state legislatures when they enacted tax obligations on the State's share of interstate commerce. . . .

It is unreasonable for companies such as Quill to invoke a "settled expectation" in conducting affairs without being taxed. Neither Quill nor any of its *amici* [friends of the Court] point to any investment decisions or reliance interests that suggest any unfairness in overturning *Bellas Hess*. And the costs of compliance with the rule, in light of today's modern computer and software technology, appear to be nominal. To the extent Quill developed any reliance on the old rule, I would submit that its reliance was unreasonable because of its failure to comply with the law as enacted by the North Dakota state legislature. Instead of rewarding companies for ignoring the studied judgments of duly elected officials, we should insist that the appropriate way to challenge a tax as unconstitutional is to pay it (or in this case collect it and remit it or place it in escrow) and then sue for declaratory judgment and refund. Quill's refusal to comply with a state tax statute prior to its being held unconstitutional hardly merits a determination that its reliance interests were reasonable. . . .

Although Congress can and should address itself to this area of law, we should not adhere to a decision, however right it was at the time, that by reason of later cases and economic reality can no longer be rationally justified. The Commerce Clause aspect of *Bellas Hess*, along with its due process holding, should be overruled.

| "The goal is to get states to voluntarily simplify their sales and use tax systems so that Congress could be persuaded to legislatively overturn Quill."

States Should Simplify Tax Laws So *Quill* Can Be Overturned

Chris Atkins

Chris Atkins was a staff attorney for the Tax Foundation in Washington, D.C. In the following viewpoint he explains that state courts have been inconsistent in how they have interpreted Quill v. North Dakota *and have ruled differently about what constitutes a retailer's physical presence in a state. In the case of the online bookseller Borders, the state ruled that because its sister company that operated Borders' physical stores promoted the Web store and accepted returns of merchandise bought online, it had to collect sales tax even though the company itself had no physical presence in the state. In other cases the outcome has been different. Therefore, says Atkins, there is a need for federal legislation. Some, but not all, states have conformed their laws to the Streamlined Sales and Use Tax Agreement with the goal of persuading Congress to enact legislation that will allow* Quill *to be overturned.*

The issue of sales and use tax collection on remote sales has plagued policymakers since the proliferation of catalog sales in the 20th century and continues to do so with the

Chris Atkins, "Establishing Physical Presence: Borders Online Case Reveals Court Disharmony in Applying Physical Presence Rules to State Sales Taxes," *State Tax Notes*, September 26, 2006. Reproduced by permission.

expansion of sales made over the Internet. The issue involves competing principles of federalism, state sovereignty, and tax neutrality.

Theoretically, all sales in a state should be taxed equally, regardless of whether the goods are purchased over the Internet or at the local shop. There is a real danger, however, in allowing state governments to make out-of-state retailers their tax collection agents. Should a state's ability to efficiently administer its sales and use tax system trump a retailer's right to freely engage in interstate commerce? Do retailers that sell and ship products from out of state receive sufficient benefits to require them to collect sales or use tax? Those questions have not yet been answered to the satisfaction of state revenue officials or the business community, who are working together on the Streamlined Sales Tax Project [SSTP] to develop a better state sales tax system.

In the 109th Congress, Sens. Michael B. Enzi, R-Wyo., and Byron Dorgan, D-N.D., introduced legislation that would give congressional approval to the SSTP system. The Sales Tax Fairness and Simplification Act (STFSA) would approve state participation in the system if a state met specified requirements. Most significantly, the legislation would overturn an important U.S. Supreme Court decision that protects remote sellers.

In the case of *Quill v. North Dakota*, the Supreme Court ruled that a remote seller could not be required to collect a state's use tax if it did not have a physical presence in that state. Last year [2005], in *Borders Online v. State Board of Equalization*, the California Court of Appeal ruled that Borders Online had to collect California use tax on all sales made to California customers. In *Borders Online*, the California appeals court ruled that Borders Online was physically present in California through its sister organization, Borders Books and Music, which had many locations in California.

Borders Online was an attempt by a state court to apply the *Quill* decision. Different state courts have interpreted *Quill* in different ways, reaching divergent conclusions about physical presence in cases with nearly identical facts. That disharmony makes the *Quill* physical presence rule ripe for clarification by Congress, which has several options in designing legislation to bring much needed clarity to that issue. Even if Congress declines to approve the STFSA, it still should clarify the physical presence rules for remote collection of state sales and use tax.

The *Borders* Case

In May 2005 the California Court of Appeal held that California could constitutionally compel Borders Online to collect use tax on products shipped into California from outside the state. In the opening paragraph of the decision, the court recognized the growing tension between sales and use tax administration and technological innovation: "We face with increasing frequency issues at the junction of Internet technology and constitutional principles. This is another such case."

At dispute in this case was whether Borders Online, which made more than $1.5 million in sales to California customers over the Internet in 1998–1999, could be required to collect and remit California use tax on those sales. Borders Online was not physically present in California (that is, it had no offices, tangible property, or employees in California). However, Borders Books and Music (a sister corporation of Borders Online) had many locations in California. Borders Inc., the parent corporation of both Borders Online and Borders Books and Music, allowed Borders Online customers to return merchandise and receive cash refunds at Borders Books and Music stores in California, and Borders Books and Music stores promoted the Borders Online Web site through general in-store advertising.

The Commerce Clause requires substantial nexus [connection] between a state and a taxpayer for the state to impose its taxing jurisdiction. In the context of collection of sales and use tax, the U.S. Supreme Court has ruled that retailers with no physical presence in a state do not have the required substantial nexus and are thus shielded from collecting use taxes on the state's behalf. Thus, Borders Online claimed that California could not constitutionally require it to collect California use tax on its sales to California customers because it had no offices, employees, or property in California.

The California Court of Appeal disagreed. The court principally relied on state law and two Supreme Court rulings on nexus in reaching its decision. Under California law, a retailer is obliged to collect use tax if it is "engaged in business in the state." California law defines "engaged in business in this state" as "any retailer having any representative, agent . . . or solicitor operating in this state . . . for the purpose of selling, delivering, installing, assembling, or . . . taking of orders for any tangible personal property." The State Board of Equalization argued that Borders Books and Music, by accepting returns of Borders Online merchandise and promoting the use of Borders Online services to the customers of Borders Stores, was acting as the agent of Borders Online. The court agreed.

Having found that Borders Books and Music was operating as Borders Online's agent, the court easily dispatched the question of physical presence. The Supreme Court has ruled that sellers that have agents acting on their behalf to establish and maintain a market in a state for sales can be subjected to the state's tax jurisdiction. Though those cases were decided before *Quill*, they dealt with the separate question of whether businesses could establish nexus through the actions of their agents or salespersons. Reading *Quill* in light of those earlier cases, the court ruled that Borders Online was physically present through the actions performed by Borders Books and

Music on its behalf (for example, giving cash refunds for returned merchandise and advertising for Borders Online).

Borders Online takes its place in a growing number of state court decisions on state sales and use tax nexus. Some state court decisions have required more substantial physical presence to impose nexus while others have allowed nexus even when the facts showed the slightest amount of physical presence. I will now review those decisions.

Relevant State Court Decisions

Several state court decisions have attempted to apply the *Quill* physical presence standard in the context of various factual circumstances, but state courts have not always decided similar cases in similar ways. . . . State courts have decided that *Quill* dictates a different outcome even when the facts of the case are almost identical.

In one case (*In re Intercard*), 11 repair visits over four years were deemed insufficient to create nexus, but in another case (*In re Orvis*), 12 visits over a three-year period were deemed sufficient to create nexus. In neither case were the employees of the retailer actually engaged in the solicitation of sales, an activity that is routinely understood to generate nexus sufficient to warrant sales or use tax collection. In fact, in . . . [most cases] the retailer's activities were limited to what we might define as customer service activities.

The courts in those cases struggled with two principal questions: first, the quality of the activities performed; second, the quantity of the activities performed. More often than not, those two questions come into conflict.

On the first question, the quality of activities, all the courts agreed that a slight physical presence (or a mere 'toe in the water') is not sufficient to meet the Supreme Court's standard in *Quill*. In other words, the definition of physical presence is not to be taken literally. If that were the case, then a retailer could be forced to collect use tax on all its sales to a state merely on the passage of its delivery truck through a state, or when one of its employees changed planes at an airport in the state. Yes, the retailer would technically be physically present in those cases, but the physical presence was not at all related to the sales activity.

The question of quality can be clearly seen in [*Arizona Department of Revenue v.*] *Care Computer Systems.* In that case, although Care's employees were not frequently present in Arizona, the court nonetheless found that their activities (solicitation, training, and leasing of property) were significant enough to find nexus.

On the second question, the quantity of activities, courts have to ask whether the presence is of sufficient quantity to require the retailer to collect use tax on all sales made to customers in the state. One can imagine a situation in which a retailer sends a technician to install purchased machinery for a customer on only one occasion. It would make no sense to force the retailer to collect use tax on all its future sales into that state simply because of one instance of significant physical presence (a "quick dip in the water").

The question of quantity can be seen in [*Florida Department of Revenue v.*] *Share International.* In that case, although Share sold products and collected sales tax at a three-day seminar in Florida, it was at no other time physically present in Florida even though it made many sales to customers in Florida. Despite a significant, one-time example of physical presence, the Florida Supreme Court was uncomfortable in ruling that Florida could force Share to collect use tax on all its sales to Florida customers.

The Need for Federal Legislation

Unfortunately for retailers, even though all state courts agree that more than a mere physical presence is necessary, that's where the agreement ends. Thus, retailers have no idea whether sending technicians or salespersons to a state for 1, 2, or 10 days will trigger nexus. That creates uncertainty and confusion for retailers engaged in interstate commerce and begs for a legislative solution.

The SSTP is a partnership between state lawmakers, revenue officials, and business groups. The goal is to get states to voluntarily simplify their sales and use tax systems so that Congress could be persuaded to legislatively overturn *Quill* and allow states to impose use tax collection responsibility on remote sellers.

The SSTP has made significant progress thus far [as of 2006]. More than 20 states have conformed their laws (to varying degrees) to the Streamlined Sales and Use Tax Agreement (SSUTA), which attempts to create a harmonized sales and use tax system among the participating states.

> *"It is simply too administratively bur-*
> *densome to require businesses to be-*
> *come agents for local and state tax col-*
> *lectors all across the country."*

Many States Are Trying to Get Around the *Quill* Ruling

Brett Joshpe

Brett Joshpe is an attorney and author in New York City. In the following viewpoint he argues that the Internet is the invention most responsible for enhancing peoples' freedom, and yet the states and Congress are trying to make it less free. The state of New York has defied the Supreme Court's decision in Quill v. North Dakota *by passing a law requiring retailers to collect sales tax if they have affiliate advertisers in the state. The large Internet sellers Amazon and Overstock are fighting this law through litigation, but other states are considering passing similar ones, and Congress may try to pass laws permitting it. In Joshpe's opinion it would be fairer to have a uniform consumption tax that would replace income tax. Such a tax would give states needed revenues while avoiding the administrative nightmare of having out-of-state businesses collect sales taxes.*

What is the single modern invention most responsible for enhancing peoples' freedom and standard of living across the world? Arguably, it is the Internet. Yet, Democrats from revenue-starved states and Congress are proposing to make it less free by taxing Internet commerce. (Content regulation should be coming soon to a screen near you.)

Brett Joshpe, "Here Comes the Internet Tax," *American Spectator*, May 27, 2009. Copyright © The American Spectator 2009. Reproduced by permission.

This should not come as a terrible surprise. After all, the Internet was just too good, too free, too easy, too innovative, and too favorable to small businesses for government to stay away. So now, several states, and Congress, are considering laws that would require online retailers to collect state and local taxes from online consumers.

New York was the first state to pass such a law last year in defiance of the 1992 U.S. Supreme Court decision, *Quill v. North Dakota*, which held that retailers must have a physical presence within a state for that state to require sales tax collection. The decision, which was based upon the dormant commerce clause doctrine—which essentially says that Congress's power to regulate interstate commerce implicitly denies such power to the states—upheld a bright line physical presence test. It also held that only Congress, through legislation, could delegate broader powers to the states.

New York's legislation attempted to end run around *Quill* by requiring online retailers to collect state and local sales tax if they had affiliate advertisers within the state. (It depends on what the meaning of *physical presence* is.) Affiliate advertisers basically consist of websites, often run by small businesses or organizations like the Parent Teacher's Association, that carry advertisements from other online retailers, like Overstock.com or Amazon.com. As a result of the massive administrative costs that the law would have imposed, Overstock.com immediately terminated its relationship with approximately 3,400 affiliates. Jonathan Johnson, Overstock.com's president, explained that "New York's law made the cost of doing business with affiliates based in New York prohibitively high."

Overstock.com and Amazon are now litigating the constitutionality of the New York law before the New York Appellate Division, but other states are considering passing similar laws in order to generate more tax revenue. Thus far, opponents have succeeded in defeating these proposals in many states where they have been proposed, although the Hawaii and

Minnesota legislatures recently passed Internet sales tax bills that still must be signed into law. However, the real fight appears headed for Congress, where proposed legislation would allow states that are part of the Streamlined Sales Tax Project (designed to simplify state tax collection) to force online retailers to collect state sales tax.

A Burden for Online Retailers

As part of the growing co-dependency of big government and big business, the National Federation of Retailers supports the tax, since it would significantly burden pesky online competitors who provide consumers with lower priced products. And proponents of the proposed federal law argue that it would not significantly increase the burden of online retailers to collect state and local taxes. However, despite the Streamlined Sales Tax Project, online retailers could still be forced to collect taxes under thousands of separate tax regimes—something that would be technologically difficult and very expensive for many smaller online businesses.

Currently, consumers who purchase online products are required in many cases to report those purchases and pay sales tax on their own. Of course, most do not. And the high rate of non-compliance should raise questions about the entire sales tax regime as it exists, especially *vis-à-vis* the Internet, which has been a boon for smaller businesses and consumers.

It is simply too administratively burdensome to require businesses to become agents for local and state tax collectors all across the country. Similarly, it is as ridiculous to expect consumers to monitor and report online purchases as it is to expect babysitters to report their income to the IRS.

Uniform Federal Tax Would Be Fair

If the government wants to impose a sales tax on consumers who purchase products online, there is a simple, fair, and efficient way of doing so: pass a federal FAIR Tax law that establishes a uniform consumption tax rate in place of the current income tax regime. Doing so would balance administrative feasibility with the need for government revenue, without destroying incentives to do business.

That, however, is not happening in the current political environment. They always say freedom isn't free. Lawmakers throughout the country are once again proving that adage accurate.

> "The Amazon Tax is unconstitutional. It hurts businesses, charities, and bloggers."

Quill Was Sound and Should Not Be Overturned

D. Dowd Muska

D. Dowd Muska is a writer, commentator, and lecturer. In the following viewpoint he argues that the Quill *ruling made sense at the time it was issued and that it was unfortunate that the Court left the door open for Congress to pass laws requiring sellers to remit sales taxes to states with which they have no connection. The Streamlined Sales and Use Tax Agreement (SSUTA), through which the states hope to encourage Congress to pass such a law, is a failure, he says, because after a decade only twenty-three states have brought their tax structure into conformance with it. Instead, states are now approving what has become known as the Amazon Tax, a scheme to collect sales taxes from Internet sellers such as Amazon.com who pay royalties to Web sites that bring customers to them through links. In Muska's opinion these laws are not allowed under* Quill *and hurt many people. He predicts that his own state legislators in Connecticut will nevertheless pass such a law.*

Drenched-in-denial pols [politicians] are adept at using every tool available to wish away Connecticut's dire fiscal condition. They've raised corporate and income taxes, adopted too-rosy economic projections, grabbed federal cash, borrowed billions, "securitized" future funding sources, and drained the budget reserve.

D. Dowd Muska, "Connecticut and the 'Amazon Tax': A Natural Fit," DowdMuska.com, March 25, 2010. Reproduced by permission.

What's on deck? The "Amazon Tax."

Since the dawn of Internet shopping, state governments' revenue-mongers have seethed that most online purchases are not subject to sales taxes. A 1992 U.S. Supreme Court decision, *Quill Corp. v. North Dakota*, held that there is no obligation to collect tax on items bought by customers living in states where vendors do not have stores, offices, warehouses, or salesmen. The ruling was founded on the Commerce Clause of the U.S. Constitution, which grants the federal government sole authority to regulate interstate trade. Thus, Connecticut cannot force a Texas-based outlet to place a 6 percent levy on orders shipped to the Nutmeg State. (At income-tax time, residents are legally bound to pay a "use tax" on products they obtained out of state during the previous year. The people who actually do are as numerous as the number of drivers who obey the Merritt Parkway's speed limit.)

The *Quill* Ruling Made Sense

Quill made a lot of sense. Since the New Deal, the Commerce Clause has been used to justify never-ending federal meddling in what should be purely private economic exchanges. But its original intent, to preclude state-level protectionism that promised to stifle growth in the early Republic, was sound.

Unfortunately, justices left the door open for the day when sellers would be required to remit taxes to states they have no connection to, and from which they derive no "public services." Congress "has the ultimate power to resolve" the issue, the High Court ruled, and [federal politicians] were "free to decide whether, when and to what extent the States may burden interstate mail-order concerns with a duty to collect [sales] taxes."

In the 1990s, Washington was comfortable with the status quo. The states? Not a chance. They hashed out the Streamlined Sales and Use Tax Agreement (SSUTA), an elaborate scheme to "simplify sales and use tax collection and administration" in order to ensure "that all retailers can conduct their business in a fair, competitive environment." Translation: We've found a way to get our "missing" revenue.

By signing on to the SSUTA, states agree to accept "harmonization" rules, including the removal of exemptions based on price. A "level playing field," SSUTA supporters believe, combined with sophisticated software that identifies buyers' sales-tax rates, will resolve complexity issues, and justify congressional approval of the compact.

In a word, the SSUTA is a bust. It's a decade old, and only 23 states have passed legislation to bring their states into conformance with the agreement's provisions. (Deep-blue [strongly Democratic] Connecticut isn't one of them.)

And that brings us to the Amazon Tax.

"Amazon Tax" Is Unconstitutional

Two years ago [in 2008], New York found a loophole it thinks frees the state from *Quill's* restrictions. Under the company's "Associates Program," any approved website can post Amazon advertisements. If someone visits your website (be it a blog, business, or nonprofit), then clicks on an Amazon ad that ultimately leads to a sale, you get a royalty.

Unwilling to kick their overspending habit, pols and revenucrats got to thinking: Aren't a lot of those Amazon-affiliated websites located in the Empire State [New York]? And since they are, doesn't that mean—under what the Tax Foundation calls "a nebulous, arbitrary standard of 'economic presence'"—that Amazon can be forced to collect sales tax?

Legislators decided it was worth a try. They approved what's now known as the Amazon Tax. (The e-superstore, headquartered in Seattle, is fighting the law in court, claiming it is "invalid, illegal, and unconstitutional" under both the U.S. Constitution and Constitution of the State of New York.) The *New York Times* cheered. North Carolina and Rhode Island enacted similar measures.

A bill to implement the Amazon Tax is before the Connecticut General Assembly's finance committee. If solons [legislators] approve the tax—either this legislative session or during one of the multiple special sessions sure to come as the budget crisis drags on—Amazon might not file a lawsuit. It could do here what it and other e-commerce giants have done elsewhere, and eliminate their advertising-affiliate programs.

The Amazon Tax is unconstitutional. It hurts businesses, charities, and bloggers. Many economists say its value as a revenue-raiser is dubious. It distracts Connecticut's budget debate from the urgent need to reduce expenditures.

The Amazon Tax is a disaster in every conceivable way. Prediction: Sometime soon, it will pass the [Connecticut] legislature by a wide margin.

CHAPTER 4

Tribal Land That Has Been Owned by Non-Indians Is Not Tax-Exempt

Case Overview

City of Sherrill v. Oneida Indian Nation (2005)

Over two centuries ago, beginning in 1795, the state of New York purchased more than three hundred thousand acres of land from the Oneida Indians. This was a violation of federal law, since the newly ratified Constitution specified that only the federal government could deal with the Indians, and under a 1788 treaty the land had been reserved to the Oneida "forever." But in the early years of the United States, opening land to white settlement was encouraged, and so the federal government raised no objection.

Most of the Oneida moved west, and by the 1840s only a few hundred of them remained in New York. From the late nineteenth century on, the Oneidas initiated various lawsuits in an attempt to obtain compensation for the loss of their ancestral lands. Finally, in the 1990s, the tribe bought pieces of land in New York from the private parties who then owned it, paying fair market value. They believed that because this land was within the boundaries of their original reservation, they did not owe state or local taxes on it. When Sherrill, a small city in which some of the land was located, sent them property tax bills, they refused to pay, and when Sherrill tried to evict them from the property, they sued. The lower courts ruled that their land was not taxable, so Sherrill appealed to the U.S. Supreme Court.

There was no dispute over the Oneidas' current ownership of the land. The question was whether or not it constituted "Indian Country," a legal term that is defined in federal law as including "all land within the limits of any Indian reservation under the jurisdiction of the United States Government." (Although it is now customary to refer to American Indians as

Native Americans, that is a recent term; in legal documents as well as in the names of their tribes and the organizations run by them, they are still called Indians.) Property in Indian Country is not subject to taxation or regulation by state or local governments. The Oneidas maintained that illegal transactions such as the long-ago purchase by New York could not and did not terminate their aboriginal rights in their reserved lands, even though non-Indians had owned it for many years before it was bought back.

The city of Sherrill disagreed. The property concerned was commercial property, and a decision that land could be exempted from zoning and other business regulation just by purchasing it would have a significant impact on local governments. It was not as if the Oneidas' property were a separate block of land; treating it as Indian Country would lead to scattered pieces immune from local laws in the midst of long-established communities. This would not be fair to the other property owners. "At stake here is far more than the tax status of a few parcels of land," wrote New York state in an amicus curiae (friend of the court) brief. "The Second Circuit's conclusion imperils the tax and civil regulatory jurisdiction that the State has exercised over this 250,000-plus-acre area for more than 150 years . . . thereby threatening the local tax base and financial well-being of communities in a two-county area."

Moreover, there was worry about the economic impact of Indian commercial ventures. Just outside Sherrill, the Oneida operated a high-rise gambling casino and resort that took in large sums of money—an enterprise to which more and more tribes throughout America have been turning, profitable because high-stakes gambling is banned in most states under laws that do not apply to Indian Country. Its property and sales tax status was being disputed with the county, and the resort was taking business away from merchants in the city. Yet the Oneida, though comprising less than 1 percent of the

129

area's population, had a great deal of political power. Sherrill had been advised against pursuing the suit because it was thought unlikely to win.

The Supreme Court, however, ruled eight to one in Sherrill's favor. It held that it was too late for the Oneidas to get back their tribal rights over the land, considering the long time it had been developed by others whose communities were by now well-established. It is a principle of law that if a right such as the right to property is not claimed in a timely manner, and the sudden assertion of it would cause greater problems than if it had been claimed sooner, that right may be lost. The people of Sherrill and other communities had lived there for generations with no reason to expect any reversion to Indian sovereignty over local property. Their expectations for the future could not be overridden after so long.

The Oneida still have the right to file suits seeking compensation for the original loss of their homeland, the Court pointed out. But the land they own currently is not exempt from local laws.

| "The Oneidas long ago relinquished the reins of government and cannot regain them through . . . purchases from current titleholders."

Majority Opinion: The Oneida Must Pay Property Taxes on Land They Bought Back

Ruth Bader Ginsburg

Ruth Bader Ginsburg has been a justice of the Supreme Court since 1993 and is one of its most liberal members. In the majority opinion in City of Sherrill v. Oneida Indian Nation, *she explains the history of the Oneida and the treaties that affected their occupancy of land. She then discusses other lawsuits in which they have been involved, as well as the basis of this suit. It was not until lately that they attempted to regain sovereignty over property that they bought back from private landowners, she points out, whereas for the past two centuries the land has been governed by New York state and local governments. The Court concluded that it would be impractical to change that now; and it is well-established in law that the passage of time can prevent validation of long-dormant claims.*

This case concerns properties in the city of Sherrill, New York, purchased by the Oneida Indian Nation of New York (OIN or Tribe) in 1997 and 1998. The separate parcels of

Ruth Bader Ginsburg, majority opinion, *City of Sherrill v. Oneida Indian Nation*, U.S. Supreme Court, March 29, 2005. Reproduced by permission.

land in question, once contained within the Oneidas' 300,000-acre reservation, were last possessed by the Oneidas as a tribal entity in 1805. For two centuries, governance of the area in which the properties are located has been provided by the State of New York and its county and municipal units. In *County of Oneida v. Oneida Indian Nation of N. Y.*, (1985) *(Oneida II)*, this Court held that the Oneidas stated a triable claim for damages against the County of Oneida for wrongful possession of lands they conveyed to New York State in 1795 in violation of federal law. In the instant [current] action, OIN resists the payment of property taxes to Sherrill on the ground that OIN's acquisition of fee title [ownership] to discrete parcels of historic reservation land revived the Oneidas' ancient sovereignty piecemeal over each parcel. Consequently, the Tribe maintains, regulatory authority over OINs' newly purchased properties no longer resides in Sherrill.

Our 1985 decision recognized that the Oneidas could maintain a federal common-law claim for damages for ancient wrongdoing in which both national and state governments were complicit. Today, we decline to project redress for the Tribe into the present and future, thereby disrupting the governance of central New York's counties and towns. Generations have passed during which non-Indians have owned and developed the area that once composed the Tribe's historic reservation. And at least since the middle years of the 19th century, most of the Oneidas have resided elsewhere. Given the longstanding, distinctly non-Indian character of the area and its inhabitants, the regulatory authority constantly exercised by New York State and its counties and towns, and the Oneidas' long delay in seeking judicial relief against parties other than the United States, we hold that the Tribe cannot unilaterally revive its ancient sovereignty, in whole or in part, over the parcels at issue. The Oneidas long ago relinquished the reins of government and cannot regain them through open-market purchases from current titleholders.

History of the Oneida Indian Nation

OIN is a federally recognized Indian Tribe and a direct descendant of the Oneida Indian Nation (Oneida Nation), "one of the six nations of the Iroquois, the most powerful Indian Tribe in the Northeast at the time of the American Revolution." At the birth of the United States, the Oneida Nation's aboriginal homeland comprised some six million acres in what is now central New York.

In the years after the Revolutionary War, "the State of New York came under increasingly heavy pressure to open the Oneidas' land for settlement." *Oneida II*. Reflective of that pressure, in 1788, New York State and the Oneida Nation entered into the Treaty of Fort Schuyler. For payments in money, and kind, the Oneidas ceded to New York "all their lands." Of the vast area conveyed, "[t]he Oneidas retained a reservation of about 300,000 acres," *Oneida II*, "for their own use and cultivation," OIN does not here contest the legitimacy of the Fort Schuyler conveyance or the boundaries of the reserved area.

The Federal Government initially pursued a policy protective of the New York Indians, undertaking to secure the Tribes' rights to reserved lands. In 1790, Congress passed the first Indian Trade and Intercourse Act, commonly known as the Nonintercourse Act. Periodically renewed, and remaining substantially in force today, the Act bars sales of tribal land without the acquiescence of the Federal Government. In 1794, in further pursuit of its protective policy, the United States entered into the Treaty of Canandaigua with the Six (Iroquois) Nations. That treaty both "acknowledge[d]" the Oneida Reservation as established by the Treaty of Fort Schuyler and guaranteed the Oneidas' "free use and enjoyment" of the reserved territory. The Oneidas in turn agreed they would "never claim any other lands within the boundaries of the United States."

New York State nonetheless continued to purchase reservation land from the Oneidas. . . .

The Federal Government's policy soon veered away from protection of New York and other east coast reservations. In lieu of the commitment made in the Treaty of Canandaigua, the United States pursued a policy designed to open reservation lands to white settlers and to remove tribes westward. . . .

Pressured by the removal policy to leave their ancestral lands in New York, some 150 Oneidas, by 1825, had moved to Wisconsin. In 1838, the Oneidas and the United States entered into the Treaty of Buffalo Creek, which envisioned removal of all remaining New York Indians, including the Oneidas, to Kansas. By this time, the Oneidas had sold all but 5,000 acres of their original reservation. Six hundred of their members resided in Wisconsin, while 620 remained in New York State.

In Article 13 of the Buffalo Creek Treaty, the Oneidas agreed to remove to the Kansas lands the United States had set aside for them "as soon as they c[ould] make satisfactory arrangements" for New York State's "purchase of their lands at Oneida." . . . Commissioner Ransom H. Gillet, who had originally negotiated the treaty terms with the Oneidas, met with them again and assured them they would not be forced to move but could remain on "their lands *where they reside*," i.e., they could "if they ch[ose] to do so remain *where they are* forever." (emphases added).

The Oneidas who stayed on in New York after the proclamation of the Buffalo Creek Treaty continued to diminish in number and, during the 1840's, sold most of their remaining lands to the State. By 1920, only 32 acres continued to be held by the Oneidas. . . .

Previous Lawsuits by the Oneidas

In 1970, the Oneidas of New York and Wisconsin, asserting federal-question jurisdiction, instituted a "test case" against the New York Counties of Oneida and Madison. They alleged that the cession of 100,000 acres to New York State in 1795, violated the Nonintercourse Act and thus did not terminate the Oneidas' right to possession under the applicable federal treaties and statutes. . . . The District Court, affirmed by the Court of Appeals, dismissed the Oneidas' complaint for failure to state a claim arising under federal law. We reversed that determination, holding that federal jurisdiction was properly invoked.

In the next round, the Oneidas prevailed in the lower courts. On review in *Oneida II*, we rejected various defenses the counties presented that might have barred the action for damages, and held that the Oneidas could maintain their claim to be compensated "for violation of their possessory rights based on federal common law." . . .

The Oneidas further sought to enlarge the action by demanding recovery of land they had not occupied since the 1795–1846 conveyances. They attempted to join [include] as defendants, *inter alia* [among others], approximately 20,000 private landowners, and to obtain declaratory relief that would allow the Oneidas to eject these landowners. The District Court refused permission to join the landowners so late in the day, resting in part on the Oneidas' bad faith and undue delay. Further, the court found the proposed amendment "futile." In this regard, the court emphasized the "sharp distinction between the *existence* of a federal common law right to Indian homelands," a right this Court recognized in *Oneida II*, "and how to *vindicate* that right." That distinction "must be drawn," the court stated, for in the two centuries since the alleged wrong, "development of every type imaginable has been ongoing." Referring to the "practical concerns" that blocked restoration of Indians to their former lands, the court found it high time "to transcend the theoretical." Cases of this genre, the court observed, "cr[ied] out for a pragmatic approach." The District Court therefore excluded the imposition of any liability against private landowners.

The Present Situation

This brings us to the present case, which concerns parcels of land in the city of Sherrill, located in Oneida County, New York. According to the 2000 census, over 99% of the population in the area is non-Indian: American Indians represent less than 1% of the city of Sherrill's population and less than 0.5% of Oneida County's population. OIN owns approximately 17,000 acres of land scattered throughout the Counties of Oneida and Madison, representing less than 1.5% of the counties' total area. OIN's predecessor, the Oneida Nation, had transferred the parcels at issue to one of its members in 1805, who sold the land to a non-Indian in 1807. The properties thereafter remained in non-Indian hands until OIN's acquisitions in 1997 and 1998 in open-market transactions. OIN now operates commercial enterprises on these parcels: a gasoline station, a convenience store, and a textile facility.

Because the parcels lie within the boundaries of the reservation originally occupied by the Oneidas, OIN maintained that the properties are exempt from taxation, and accordingly refused to pay the assessed property taxes. The city of Sherrill initiated eviction proceedings in state court, and OIN sued Sherrill in federal court. In contrast to *Oneida I* and *II*, which involved demands for monetary compensation, OIN sought equitable relief prohibiting, currently and in the future, the imposition of property taxes. OIN also sued Madison County, seeking a declaration that the Tribe's properties in Madison are tax exempt. The litigation involved a welter of claims and counterclaims. Relevant here, the District Court concluded that parcels of land owned by the Tribe in Sherrill and Madison are not taxable.

A divided panel of the Second Circuit affirmed. Writing for the majority, Judge [Barrington] Parker ruled that the parcels qualify as "Indian country," as that term is defined in [the law], because they fall within the boundaries of a reservation set aside by the 1794 Canandaigua Treaty for Indian use under federal supervision. . . .

OIN and the United States argue that because the Court in *Oneida II* recognized the Oneidas' aboriginal title to their ancient reservation land and because the Tribe has now acquired the specific parcels involved in this suit in the open market, it has unified fee and aboriginal title and may now assert sovereign dominion over the parcels. . . .

In this action, OIN seeks declaratory and injunctive relief [a ruling stating that the taxes are not owed and forbidding the city from assessing them] recognizing its present and future sovereign immunity from local taxation on parcels of land the Tribe purchased in the open market, properties that had been subject to state and local taxation for generations. We now reject the unification theory of OIN and the United States and hold that "standards of federal Indian law and federal equity practice" preclude the Tribe from rekindling embers of sovereignty that long ago grew cold.

Too Late to Regain Sovereignty

The appropriateness of the relief OIN here seeks must be evaluated in light of the long history of state sovereign control over the territory. From the early 1800's into the 1970's, the United States largely accepted, or was indifferent to, New York's governance of the land in question and the validity *vel non* [or not] of the Oneidas' sales to the State. In fact, the United States' policy and practice through much of the early 19th century was designed to dislodge east coast lands from Indian possession. Moreover, the properties here involved have greatly increased in value since the Oneidas sold them 200 years ago. Notably, it was not until lately that the Oneidas sought to regain ancient sovereignty over land converted from wilderness to become part of cities like Sherrill. . . .

The wrongs of which OIN complains in this action occurred during the early years of the Republic. For the past two centuries, New York and its county and municipal units have continuously governed the territory. The Oneidas did not seek to regain possession of their aboriginal lands by court decree until the 1970's. And not until the 1990's did OIN acquire the properties in question and assert its unification theory to ground its demand for exemption of the parcels from local taxation. This long lapse of time, during which the Oneidas did not seek to revive their sovereign control through equitable relief in court, and the attendant dramatic changes in the character of the properties, preclude OIN from gaining the disruptive remedy it now seeks.

The principle that the passage of time can preclude relief has deep roots in our law, and this Court has recognized this prescription in various guises. It is well established that laches [negligence in asserting a legal right], a doctrine focused on one side's inaction and the other's legitimate reliance, may bar long-dormant claims for equitable relief. . . .

This Court's original-jurisdiction state-sovereignty cases do not dictate a result here, but they provide a helpful point of reference: When a party belatedly asserts a right to present and future sovereign control over territory, longstanding observances and settled expectations are prime considerations. There is no dispute that it has been two centuries since the Oneidas last exercised regulatory control over the properties here or held them free from local taxation. Parcel-by-parcel revival of their sovereign status, given the extraordinary passage of time, would dishonor "the historic wisdom in the value of repose." *Oneida II.*

Finally, this Court has recognized the impracticability of returning to Indian control land that generations earlier passed into numerous private hands. The District Court, in the litigation dormant during the pendency of *Oneida II*, rightly found these pragmatic concerns about restoring Indian sovereign control over land "magnified exponentially here, where development of every type imaginable has been ongoing for more than two centuries."

In this case, the Court of Appeals concluded that the "impossibility" doctrine had no application because OIN acquired the land in the open market and does not seek to uproot current property owners. But the unilateral reestablishment of present and future Indian sovereign control, even over land purchased at the market price, would have disruptive practical consequences similar to those that led this Court in *Yankton Sioux* to initiate the impossibility doctrine. The city of Sherrill and Oneida County are today overwhelmingly populated by non-Indians. A checkerboard of alternating state and tribal jurisdiction in New York State—created unilaterally at OIN's behest—would "seriously burde[n] the administration of state and local governments" and would adversely affect landowners neighboring the tribal patches. If OIN may unilaterally reassert sovereign control and remove these parcels from the local tax rolls, little would prevent the Tribe from initiating a new generation of litigation to free the parcels from local zoning or other regulatory controls that protect all landowners in the area. . . .

In sum, the question of damages for the Tribe's ancient dispossession is not at issue in this case, and we therefore do not disturb our holding in *Oneida II*. However, the distance from 1805 to the present day, the Oneidas' long delay in seeking equitable relief against New York or its local units, and developments in the city of Sherrill spanning several generations, evoke the doctrines of laches, acquiescence, and impossibility, and render inequitable the piecemeal shift in governance this suit seeks unilaterally to initiate.

| "*[The Court's] decision today is at war with at least two bedrock principles of Indian law.*"

Dissenting Opinion: Only Congress Can Revoke Immunity of Indian Land from Taxation

John Paul Stevens

John Paul Stevens was, at his retirement on June 29, 2010, the oldest and longest-serving member (since 1975) then sitting on the Supreme Court and was generally considered to be the leader of its liberal faction. In the following dissenting opinion in City of Sherrill v. Oneida Indian Nation, *he argues that it is clear that the land owned by the Oneida Indian tribe is within the boundaries of its original reservation and that it therefore qualifies as "Indian Country" not subject to taxation. Only Congress has the power to diminish a reservation, he says, and the Court should not have taken action that effectively does so. In his opinion, to deny the tribe its fundamental rights over land that it reacquired by purchase is both inequitable and a violation of the law.*

Since the outset of this litigation it has been common ground that if the Tribe's properties are "Indian Country," the City has no jurisdiction to tax them without express congressional consent. For the reasons set forth at length in the opinions of the District Court and the Court of Appeals, it is

John Paul Stevens, dissenting opinion, *City of Sherrill v. Oneida Indian Nation*, U.S. Supreme Court, March 29, 2005. Reproduced by permission.

abundantly clear that all of the land owned by the Tribe within the boundaries of its reservation qualifies as Indian country. Without questioning the accuracy of that conclusion, the Court today nevertheless decides that the fact that most of the reservation has been occupied and governed by non-Indians for a long period of time precludes the Tribe "from rekindling embers of sovereignty that long ago grew cold." This is a novel holding, and in my judgment even more unwise than the Court's holding in *County of Oneida v. Oneida Indian Nation of N. Y.* (1985), that the Tribe may recover damages for the alleged illegal conveyance of its lands that occurred in 1795. In that case, I argued that the "remedy for the ancient wrong established at trial should be provided by Congress, not by judges seeking to rewrite history at this late date." In the present case, the Tribe is not attempting to collect damages or eject landowners as a remedy for a wrong that occurred centuries ago; rather, it is invoking an ancient immunity against a city's present-day attempts to tax its reservation lands.

Only Congress Can Remove Immunity

Without the benefit of relevant briefing from the parties, the Court has ventured into legal territory that belongs to Congress. Its decision today is at war with at least two bedrock principles of Indian law. First, only Congress has the power to diminish or disestablish a tribe's reservation. Second, as a core incident of tribal sovereignty, a tribe enjoys immunity from state and local taxation of its reservation lands, until that immunity is explicitly revoked by Congress. Far from revoking this immunity, Congress has specifically reconfirmed it with respect to the reservation lands of the New York Indians. Ignoring these principles, the Court has done what only Congress may do—it has effectively proclaimed a diminishment of the Tribe's reservation and an abrogation of its elemental right to tax immunity. Under our precedents, whether it is wise policy to honor the Tribe's tax immunity is a question for Congress, not this Court, to decide.

As a justification for its lawmaking decision, the Court relies heavily on the fact that the Tribe is seeking *equitable* relief in the form of an injunction. The distinction between law and equity is unpersuasive because the outcome of the case turns on a narrow legal issue that could just as easily, if not most naturally, be raised by a tribe as a *defense* against a state collection proceeding. In fact, that scenario actually occurred in this case: The City brought an eviction proceeding against the Tribe based on its refusal to pay property taxes; that proceeding was removed to federal court and consolidated with the present action; the District Court granted summary judgment for the Tribe; and the Court of Appeals affirmed on the basis of tribal tax immunity. Either this defensive use of tax immunity should still be available to the Tribe on remand, or the Court's reliance on the distinctions between law and equity and between substantive rights and remedies, is indefensible.

In any event, as a matter of equity I believe that the "principle that the passage of time can preclude relief," should be applied sensibly and with an even hand. It seems perverse to hold that the reliance interests of non-Indian New Yorkers that are predicated on almost two centuries of inaction by the Tribe do not foreclose the Tribe's enforcement of judicially created damages remedies for ancient wrongs, but do somehow mandate a forfeiture of a tribal immunity that has been consistently and uniformly protected throughout our history. In this case, the Tribe reacquired reservation land in a peaceful and lawful manner that fully respected the interests of innocent landowners—it purchased the land on the open market. To now deny the Tribe its right to tax immunity—at once the most fundamental of tribal rights and the least disruptive to other sovereigns—is not only inequitable, but also irreconcilable with the principle that only Congress may abrogate or extinguish tribal sovereignty. I would not decide this case on the basis of speculation about what may happen in future litigation over other regulatory issues. For the answer to the question whether the City may require the Tribe to pay taxes on its own property within its own reservation is pellucidly [quite transparently] clear. Under settled law, it may not.

Accordingly, I respectfully dissent.

> "Pretending that reservation boundaries that were drawn in the 1780s are still in effect today . . . would be like pretending that England never lost the colonies."

The Oneida Have Lost All Claims to Sovereignty

Charles G. Curtis Jr. et al.

Attorney Charles G. Curtis Jr. represented several towns in New York state that filed an amici curiae (friends of the court) brief supporting the city of Sherrill. In the following portion of the brief, he argues that creating a checkerboard of "Indian Country" exempt from taxes would have a serious impact on the area and lead to conflicts between state and federal jurisdiction. To pretend the events of the last two centuries never happened, he says, would be like saying that England, France and Spain still have rights on the North American continent. He maintains that the Oneida are entitled to monetary damages for any treaty violations they can prove, but that they have lost the right to sovereignty over pieces of land in the middle of established communities.

"When an area is predominately populated by non-Indians with only a few surviving pockets of Indian allotments, finding that the land remains Indian country seriously burdens the administration of State and local governments." *Solem v. Bartlett* (1984). The first two *amici* are towns within the area encompassed by the historic boundaries of the

Charles G. Curtis Jr. et al., brief of *amici curiae* Town of Lenox, New York, et al., *City of Sherrill v. Oneida Indian Nation*, U.S. Supreme Court, 2005. Reproduced by permission.

Oneida's 18th-century reservations—boundaries that have been treated as having been extinguished since at least the Jacksonian era. These *amici* and other area local governments have struggled in recent years to carry out their responsibilities in the face of unilateral attempts by the Oneida Indian Nation of New York to withdraw increasing amounts of purchased land from state and local taxation, zoning, and other regulatory oversight—all on the premise that the 18th-century reservation boundaries have never been diminished to *any* extent and that the entire area is now and always has been "Indian country." The other *amicus* is a town located outside the boundaries of the Oneida land claim area, but which is keenly interested in the rules of present-day sovereignty and jurisdiction that apply in areas subject to ancient tribal claims.

The Oneida's unilateral attempts to withdraw lands from the local tax base have had a serious impact on the *amici*'s budgets and services in recent years. In addition, as this Court has recognized, creating "Indian country" sovereignty in "scattered checkerboard fashion over a territory otherwise under state jurisdiction" will "obviously" result in "many practical and legal conflicts between state and federal jurisdiction with regard to conduct and parties having mobility over the checkerboard territory." *DeCoteau v. District County Court for the Tenth Judicial Dist.* (1975). This is particularly so where, as here, the layout of the checkerboard is left entirely to the discretion of the [Oneida] Nation; sovereignty, jurisdiction, and regulatory authority over any given parcel of land supposedly change hands simply through an open-market transaction. This has resulted in the Nation being able to cherry pick whatever lands it wishes—including gas stations, convenience stores, shopping centers, marinas, and other key commercial properties—and then unilaterally purporting to declare their immunity from state and local taxation and regulation. It is difficult if not impossible for local governments to carry out their home rule powers and statutory mandates in the midst of the ensuing chaos and uncertainty.

Two Centuries Cannot Be Ignored

As Senior Judge [Neal Peter] McCurn emphasized in his path-marking opinion on claims against private landowners in the Oneida land claim area, "the real task at hand" is to determine "how, in the 21st century, to reconcile the Indians' interest in their homelands with those of current landowners who, understandably, also view the claim area as their 'homeland.'" *Oneida Indian Nation of New York State v. County of Oneida.* It has been eight generations since the United States and the Oneida entered into the Treaty of Buffalo Creek of January 15, 1838. To treat the Oneida's *entire* 18th-century reservation as having escaped the effects of the 1838 removal treaty and as still being "Indian country" today is to pretend that the events of the last two centuries did not occur. It ignores the purpose and effect of Indian removal—the official law of the land for much of the 19th century. It ignores the language and clear Congressional purposes behind the 1838 treaty. It ignores the facts that about 85% of the Oneida people *did* leave New York during the removal era, that only about 5% of the Oneida people live there today, and that the current population of the area embraced by the old reservation boundaries is over 99% non-Oneida. And it ignores the last 166 years of "jurisdictional history," in which the federal government has *consistently* until recent years recognized state and local sovereignty over the lands in issue, with the exception of the dwindling number of tribal allotments that remained in trust.

Indian nations, no less than other sovereigns, are subject to the rule that "[l]ong acquiescence in the possession of territory and the exercise of dominion and sovereignty over it may have a controlling effect in the determination of a disputed boundary." *Massachusetts v. New York,* (1926). Pretending that reservation boundaries that were drawn in the 1780s are *still* in effect today without any adjustment—unfair and tragic though the intervening centuries have been in so many respects—would be like pretending that England never lost the colonies, that the Dutch never lost New York to the English, or that France and Spain have rights today on the North American continent.

Respecting long-established patterns of sovereignty, jurisdiction, and regulatory authority does not leave the Oneida without a means of either recovering for any treaty violations they are able to demonstrate in the ongoing land claim litigation or establishing sovereignty over recently purchased lands. As Senior Judge McCurn held on remand from this Court's decision in *County of Oneida v. Oneida Indian Nation of New York State* (1985) [*"Oneida II"*], the Oneida are entitled to recover historically adjusted monetary damages for any treaty violations they are able to establish (subject to various pending defenses and counterclaims that are presently being litigated). . . .

Particularly in light of the eight generations of delay since the 1838 treaty and the reliance interests of the many other stakeholders in the land claim area, there is no good reason to recognize the Oneida's unilateral attempts to exercise self-help remedies in the midst of ongoing litigation in which the underlying merits have yet to be resolved. If the Oneida's sovereign landbase is to be rebuilt, it must be pursuant to the intergovernmental planning mechanisms created under [federal law], not through unilateral declarations of sovereignty over checkerboard acquisitions that are cherry-picked off the open market. . . .

The Oneida's agreement with the federal government in 1838 was to remove west "as soon as they can make satisfactory arrangements with the Governor of the State of New York for the purchase of their lands at Oneida"—language that, they were told, would allow them to remain "where they *reside*" and "where they *are* forever," if "satisfactory arrangements" could not be made. (emphasis added). Even giving this language its most generous reasonable construction, the deal struck through the treaty negotiations was that the Oneida could remain "where they *are*" and "where they *reside*" (*i.e.*, on the 5,000 acres they still possessed in 1838), not that they could *reassert* rights in the 295,000 acres they had given up in recent generations. The Oneida who stayed in New York never thereafter sought to exercise possession or sovereignty over lands their forebears had previously conveyed. They thereby lost any remaining rights they may have held in these lands through acquiescence, abandonment, and relinquishment every bit as much as the Oneida who moved away from New York.

"The actual goal of New York ... is to retain the long-term benefits of their illegal conduct—the ability to tax ... tribal lands in the Oneida reservation."

The State Should Not Retain the Ability to Tax Illegally Acquired Indian Lands

Carter G. Phillips et al.

Carter G. Phillips was one of the attorneys representing the National Congress of American Indians (NCAI), which filed an amicus curiae (friend of the court) brief supporting the Oneida Indian Nation in City of Sherrill v. Oneida Indian Nation. *In the following portion of the brief, Carter and his colleagues argue that because the state of New York's original purchase of Oneida land was illegal under federal law, their tribal rights were restored when they bought it back. The city's arguments against this view are invalid. Furthermore, in NCAI's opinion the claim that a ruling against would have dire consequences for the city are greatly exaggerated, as the tribe has offered grant money equivalent to the amount of the lost taxes, which the city has refused to accept.*

This case calls for the straightforward application of long-standing principles regarding treaty interpretation and tribal tax immunity. However, the City of Sherrill argues against the application of those principles based on vastly exaggerated claims of the hardship allegedly resulting from an

Carter G. Phillips et al., brief of *amicus curiae* National Council of American Indians, *City of Sherrill v. Oneida Indian Nation*, U.S. Supreme Court, 2005. Reproduced by permission.

adverse decision. While the practical consequences of the Court's decision here would largely be confined to New York's political subdivisions and tribes, NCAI [National Congress of American Indians] and its members have a strong interest in opposing the abandonment of time-honored principles of Indian law based on arguments properly addressed to Congress, not this Court.

Unlawfully Acquired Land

Beginning in 1795, New York purchased 300,000 acres of land reserved to the Oneida Nation ("the Oneida") in plain violation of federal law. The Oneida were thereby ousted from these lands, but never lost their treaty-protected aboriginal rights of possession. Only the United States could strip the Tribe of those rights. Between that time and the present, the lands have passed from New York to third-party purchasers.

Many eastern states that engaged in comparable courses of conduct have fashioned comprehensive land-claims solutions seeking to balance the interests of tribes and landowners potentially affected by the States' illegal actions. Congress has approved those settlements. New York, however, has refused to provide Tribes within its borders with meaningful redress for its past wrongs. Given New York's intransigence, the Oneida decided to purchase parcels of lost lands in free market transactions at fair market prices, in order to reactivate the treaty and aboriginal rights inherent in tribal possession of the parcels, including an immunity from state and local taxation.

New York, the original lawbreaker in this case, cries foul on behalf of the third-party interests created by the passage of time (of course, the Oneida paid third parties fair market price to take possession). But, the actual goal of New York and its subdivisions is to retain the long-term benefits of their illegal conduct—the ability to tax not only non-Indian lands but also tribal lands in the Oneida reservation. At the end of the day, New York and its subdivisions should not be permitted to retain the fruits of their defiance of federal law, and the Oneida's reacquisition of wrongfully transferred lands in the reservation should restore those parcels' tax-immune status.

Absent express congressional authorization, state and local governments may not tax tribal lands in an Indian reservation. The parcels at issue are owned by the Oneida; they constitute part of the land "reserved" to the Oneida "forever" in the 1788 Treaty of Fort Schuyler ("1788 Treaty"). In the 1794 Treaty of Canandaigua ("1794 Treaty"), the United States "acknowledge[d]" these lands "to be [the Oneida's] property" and promised that the same "reservation shall remain theirs, until they choose to sell the same to the people of the United States, who have the right to purchase." The United States has never terminated the reservation.

"Despite Congress' clear policy" to the contrary, between 1795 and 1846, New York entered into a series of transactions through which it acquired most of the Oneida reservation, including the parcels at issue. With a single exception not relevant here, these transactions occurred without the consent of the United States. To regain possession of these parcels, the Oneida paid fair market value to non-Indian landowners in free market transactions. These facts should end this matter. Illegal transactions cannot and did not terminate the Oneida's aboriginal rights in their reserved lands, as this Court has already made clear. Thus, once the Tribe regained possession, its treaty and aboriginal rights were reinvigorated, including the parcels' immunity from state and local taxation.

Sherrill, however, claims that it may tax the parcels at issue for several reasons: (a) The lands were never part of a federal reservation and are not otherwise within Indian country as defined by federal law; (b) assuming the lands are part of a federal reservation and are now tribal lands, they are freely alienable [transferrable to another's ownership] and thus subject to state and local taxation; and (c) assuming the lands

151

were part of a federal reservation, that reservation was diminished or disestablished by the 1838 Treaty of Buffalo Creek.

NCAI agrees with respondents that Sherrill's first two arguments are answered in large part by *Oneida Indian Nation v. County of Oneida*, (1974) ("*Oneida I*") and *Oneida II*, where this Court found that after adoption of the Constitution and enactment of the Trade and Intercourse Act of 1790 (known as the "Nonintercourse Act"), sales of land in the precise area were unlawful absent federal consent. . . .

European Concepts of Ownership

When the European powers "discovered" North America and entered into their relationships with North American tribes, the "discovery doctrine" was the international law principle which reconciled European concepts of land ownership and sovereignty with aboriginal possession. Pursuant to this doctrine, discovering European nations possessed the right to exclude other European powers from discovered lands and the exclusive rights to purchase Indian lands and to extinguish aboriginal title. The tribes lost their sovereign right to conduct foreign relations with other European nations and the right independently to alienate their lands. Otherwise, the tribes retained sovereignty in their territory and an aboriginal right of occupation "as sacred and as securely safeguarded as is fee simple absolute title." *United States v. Shoshone Tribe of Indians* (1938).

The United States Constitution incorporated discovery doctrine principles by centralizing in the federal government the exclusive authority to conduct relations with tribes, including the right to extinguish Indian title and allow the alienation of tribal lands. The Constitution

"confers on Congress the powers of war and peace; of making treaties, and of regulating commerce with foreign nations, and among the several states, and with the Indian tribes. *These powers comprehend all that is required for the regulation of our intercourse with the Indians."* [*Worcester v. Georgia,* (1832) (emphasis supplied).]

The tribes were otherwise recognized as sovereign over their internal affairs and lands. In 1790, Congress exercised its exclusive authority by enacting the Nonintercourse Act, forbidding trade with Indians (absent federal authorization) and requiring that all sales of Indian lands be the product of a federal treaty or convention.

These principles of federal exclusivity and retained tribal sovereignty left state and local governments without jurisdiction over tribal Indians and lands within "Indian country," including jurisdiction to tax tribal lands, absent express federal authorization.

"Indian country" includes, *inter alia* [among other things] "all land within the limits of any Indian reservation under the jurisdiction of the United States Government, notwithstanding the issuance of any patent." An express congressional authorization is an absolute prerequisite to state or local taxation of *tribal* land in Indian country. The parcels at issue were "reserved" to the Oneida "forever" by the 1788 Treaty, and that reservation was "acknowledged" and affirmed by the United States in, *inter alia,* the 1794 Treaty. As this Court recognized in *Oneida II,* an illegal transaction does not alter aboriginal rights of possession; the Oneida's possessory rights persisted in the "reserved" lands unlawfully alienated without federal approval. In such circumstances, once the tribe pays non-Indian third parties fair value, the tribe's repossession of reserved aboriginal lands reactivates the lands' immunity from state and local taxation.

Sherrill's Arguments Are Not Valid

Sherrill's responses are without merit. *First,* Sherrill claims that the 1788 Treaty terminated the Oneida's aboriginal rights of possession (rather than "reserving" those rights "forever") before the Constitution was adopted (though after the requisite total of nine states, including New York, signed it), and therefore that the nascent federal government lacked authority over Oneida lands and the Nonintercourse Act never applied. Under this view, neither the 1794 Treaty nor any of the United States' other agreements with the Oneida could have established a federal Oneida reservation that is "'Indian country'" under [the law.]

This is plainly wrong. Even assuming that during the period from independence to the effective date of the Constitution, New York shared with the United States the *right* to extinguish aboriginal rights, the tribes retained those rights unless they actually were extinguished. Although New York purchased vast Oneida lands before the Constitution was adopted, the 1788 Treaty plainly did not terminate the Oneida's rights of possession in the discrete tract of land carved from the general cession, but instead explicitly "reserved" those rights "forever." . . .

Even if the 1788 Treaty had created a bizarre, new state-law property interest unrecognizable in its historical and legal context—simultaneously terminating and reserving the Oneida's rights of possession—the Constitution and the Nonintercourse Act nonetheless provided the United States with *exclusive* authority to extinguish the Oneida's retained rights. The Act forbids unauthorized sales of tribal lands, including "to any state, whether having the right of pre-emption to such lands or not." . . .

Second, Sherrill contends that, even if the parcels at issue are in a federal reservation, they are subject to state and local government taxation until the federal government sets them aside again. According to Sherrill, the lands must be taxable because they have become freely alienable; Sherrill's apparent belief is that the lands are owned by the Tribe acting just like any private participant in the commercial marketplace. The premise and conclusion of this argument are wrong.

Unlawfully-transferred reservation lands restored to tribal possession by purchase from non-Indian owners are *not* alienable without federal authorization under the plain language of the Nonintercourse Act. Moreover, . . . tribal reacquisition remedies an illegal transaction, restores a tax immunity unlawfully divested, and reactivates the Nonintercourse Act's restrictions on alienability.

Third, Sherrill contends even if the lands at issue were part of a federal reservation, the reservation was disestablished by the 1838 Treaty of Buffalo Creek. This Court, however, has refused to find that a treaty disestablishes a reservation unless the parties' agreement to do so is "'clear and plain.'" The text of the Treaty of Buffalo Creek by itself defeats Sherrill's claim that the Treaty mandated the removal of the Oneida from their New York reservation to the Kansas Territory. Moreover, in terms that could not be clearer, the government agent who negotiated the treaty assured the Oneida that they would not be compelled to remove and could "choose to . . . remain where they are forever." . . . The altered regional demographics on which Sherrill relies are the result of unlawful transactions, not the Treaty of Buffalo Creek, and cannot by themselves work a *de facto* [actual] disestablishment of a federal reservation.

Consequences Exaggerated

Sherrill and its *amici*'s [friends of the court] remaining arguments seek to portray the consequences of this case as so extreme that the Court cannot apply the federal Indian law principles that govern. Specifically, they say that state and local governments will suffer a crippling blow to their tax revenues and overall fiscal health. Putting aside the extra-legal nature of these assertions—which should be directed to Congress, not this Court—the argument suffers from several fatal flaws. Because other States facing New York's situation have settled their tribes' land claims, the practical consequences of the Court's decision are limited to New York, which could likewise enter into such an agreement. Further, this case addresses only the tax-immune status of reservations lands *possessed by the Tribe*. The Oneida do not assert a tax immunity for most of the reservation which is owned by non-Indians; and this Court has severely limited tribal jurisdiction and authorized state taxation of non-Indian reservation lands and activities. In addition, as the brief *amicus curiae* of the Puyallup and Southern Ute Tribes, and Pueblo of Acoma demonstrates, numerous tribes and state and local governments (including the Oneida) have reached agreements concerning tribal payment for government services. Sherrill should not be permitted to translate its refusal to accept such proposals into an argument that the law should be ignored. Neither law nor facts support Sherrill's alarmist rhetoric. . . .

Sherrill and its *amici* claim, in vastly overblown terms, that an adverse decision in this case will yield dire consequences. Their arguments are entirely misplaced. . . .

The impact that a reaffirmation of longstanding principles of tribal tax immunity would have on New York and its subdivisions is vastly exaggerated. Numerous states and counties have within their borders non-taxable tribal land holdings that dwarf the amount of land realistically at issue here. But while New York and its subdivisions have submitted numerous briefs *amicus curiae* to the Court, no other governmental entity has supported petitioner, suggesting they do not suffer fiscal chaos as a result of the presence of tribal land and, indeed, often thrive through contributions made by Indian tribes to their economies.

Sherrill's assertions on this subject ring particularly hollow. The Oneida Nation seeks to act fairly not only with respect to the third-party landowners from whom it purchased property, but also with regard to the counties and municipalities affected by those purchases. Accordingly, the Tribe operates a Silver Covenant Chain Grant program, providing direct grant monies to local governments and school districts based on the amount of tribal landholdings within their boundaries. In the case of county and municipal government units, those grant monies are equivalent to the taxes the Tribe would have paid on its landholdings absent its tax immunity. In the case of the school districts, the Tribe pays twice to three times as much in grants as it would in taxes. *Sherrill, however, has steadfastly refused to accept any grant monies from the Tribe.* Sherrill has elected to fight the Tribe rather than to cooperate with it, and should not be heard now to complain about the consequences of its own choice.

| "The ruling . . . will need months, per-
haps years, before its breadth and scope
can be fully understood."

The Ruling Against the Oneida Will Have Far-Reaching Consequences

Elaine Willman

Elaine Willman, who is of Cherokee ancestry, is an author, a former national chair of the Citizens Equal Rights Alliance, and a city planner and administrator. In the following viewpoint she explains the facts on which City of Sherrill v. Oneida Indian Nation *was based. Sherrill, the smallest city in New York state, takes pride in its excellent recreational facilities for residents and its zoning laws that make it a pleasant place to live. A few pieces of commercial property within its limits were owned by Oneida Indians, who maintained that they were not subject to the city's property tax or zoning, and the city felt that this was not fair to other property owners. The Oneida were operating a large nearby gambling casino and resort, which had major economic impact on the area, and they were politically powerful. Sherrill was advised not to sue because if it lost the case, many other pieces of land would not be subject to state or local taxes either. When the Supreme Court unexpectedly ruled in its favor, Willman says, it was a much-deserved and necessary victory that will have a substantial impact on other disputes involving Indian land.*

Elaine Willman, "David and Goliath: Sherrill, New York, and Turning Stone Casino," *Public Management*, August 2005. Copyright © 2005 International City/County Management Association. Reproduced by permission.

On March 29, 2005, the U.S. Supreme Court ruled, in what is being called a David-versus-Goliath scenario, on *City of Sherrill v. Oneida Indian Nation.* Sherrill, the smallest city in the state of New York at two and one-half square miles and 3,000 population, won the ruling handily. The issue was: Are fee-simple (taxable) parcels [of land] that have been acquired by an Indian tribe subject to local and state taxation, or are they tax-exempt as "Indian country"?

Located almost in the center of New York State—halfway between Syracuse and Utica—the city of Sherrill drew national attention in 2005 for its energetic efforts to preserve its community integrity. The diminutive town has no fewer than 10 pleasant, manicured parks to serve its people. The cheery and helpful quarterly newsletter issued from Sherrill City Hall reminds residents, "If you are going to be away for a week or more, notify the police department so that a check of your residence can be made."

Skating rinks, athletic fields, football and soccer fields, and tennis and basketball courts are well appointed and scattered throughout this small community. Sherrill's Knot Hole Club, active for more than 25 years, is solely focused on the delivery of excellent athletic and recreational programs for the nearly 1,000 young people who call Sherrill home.

"You know, we have a commitment to our citizens that when they move here, they see what they have, they know that this is a quality community and that there is zoning and we enforce our rules and regulations," said David Barker, Sherrill's city manager since 1994. "Our residents have expectations, and we meet them."

The Facts

The community is not a particularly wealthy place, with a median house-hold income of less than $50,000, but the 2000 U.S. Census reports that only seven families live below the poverty line. Sherrill is a town that takes good care of itself.

This is immediately observable to any stranger passing within the city's borders. Sherrill was the "David" in this millennium's David vs. Goliath litigation.

Not far from Sherrill, about three miles as the crow flies— rising 253 feet into the air, at 19 floors, and offering some 200,000 square feet of space containing more than 2,400 slot machines and 100 game tables—stands the Turning Stone Casino. This millennial castle of Goliath is the manifest dream of the Oneida Indian Nation of New York's (OINNY) Chief Executive Officer [CEO] Ray Halbritter.

The glistening, glass-and-mirror tower that is the Turning Stone Resort-Casino dwarfs everything around it, with the next tallest building within a radius of 40 miles being the 10-story Oneida County seat.

Annual revenue figures for the Turning Stone Casino have varied from $70 million to $167 million in recent years, with rumors of 50 percent profit margins. In its 2004 annual report, the OINNY reported that its customers' "expenditures on consumable goods and services totaled more than $342 million," or "almost one and a half times more than the amount that New York State budgets annually to run its state legislature, $200 million." This is an enormous amount of goods purchased annually, upon which little, if any, sales tax is collected or paid.

The position taken by OINNY when acquiring properties on the current tax rolls of Oneida and Madison counties is that, once acquired by the OINNY, these former "ancestral" lands become new Indian country and are therefore not subject to tax or regulation by the local, county, or state government. Halbritter takes this position one step further. Until the recent ruling, he had also refused to place 18,000 acres of noncontiguous parcels in a federal trust.

Thus, CEO Halbritter has established a veritable kingdom within the two counties that is answerable to no one—not the counties, nor the state of New York, nor the United States. It is a separate, sovereign nation that makes its own rules as it goes along and follows no one else's.

Only two of the OINNY parcels were acquired in Sherrill. The local government believed that if a couple of parcels could be purchased, more could surely follow, and the locality could become seriously disrupted by patches of Indian country that fail to comply with local tax or zoning regulations.

Litigation

In 1997, Sherrill sent a property-tax bill to OINNY, as it would every other property owner within its bounds. OINNY declined to pay the annual property taxes. As this debt to Sherrill continued in delinquency, Sherrill filed tax liens on the parcels. The city commissioners, as well as the rest of the community, stood firmly behind the city manager in all actions respecting this conflict.

In February 2000, the OINNY took Sherrill into federal court, seeking to prevent the city from collecting delinquent or future property taxes on OINNY properties. The litigation proceeded through the federal judicial system, with the city losing in the U.S. District Court in June 2001. Sherrill also was defeated in the 2nd Circuit Court of Appeals in July 2003. With some courage, the little city had pursued appeals on every decision, including its last hope—an appeal to the U.S. Supreme Court that was filed in 2004.

The Supreme Court asked a former U.S. Solicitor General, Ted Olson, for an opinion on whether the case should be heard by the Highest Court. In early June 2004, Olson advised the Supreme Court not to hear the case. On June 28, 2004, the Supreme Court decided against this advice and accepted the case for review. Sherrill would become "the little city that could."

The Standoff

This unlikely standoff between a tiny town and a politically overwhelming tribal power was flying under the radar screen of U.S. media, except for those journalists and academic specialists who closely watch federal Indian policy. The issues involved in the case held substantial consequences for both the victor and the vanquished.

City Manager David Barker said, "I have no problem, as long as the tribal businesses play by the same rules as every other corporate citizen. If they want a longhouse, if they want a museum, I have no problem with that being tax-exempt. But when they have a commercial enterprise, that is a whole different ballgame."

The lawsuit stemmed from Sherrill's determination to treat a tribal business and property in the same manner as other businesses within the city. When asked about what kind of support the city of Sherrill had been receiving regarding the litigation, Barker replied: "We were asked at various stages of the legal road to back off, by state and county officials, when we first got into this lawsuit. We were involved in a meeting in Syracuse where they asked us not to proceed, and this was . . . very early on. We were told that the county and state [were] already involved in this tax dispute.

"So I said, 'Well, we will be putting that much more pressure on it,'" Barker continued with an impish grin. "We all recognized the fact that if we lost, that would strengthen the Oneida position, and when we did lose in district court, it certainly did strengthen their position, and they became much more aggressive. But we took the case to the next step, and we lost there, too."

On the subject of the fiscal impacts of the tribe's parcels, according to Barker, "We lost about $60,900 the first year in sales-tax money. So, to cover this amount would mean a 10 percent tax increase—I mean, that's 10 percent each year! Then, the Oneidas opened other facilities, a smoke shop and a tee-shirt factory. They have a retail outlet out front. Normally, when something like that goes in, we would see our sales-tax revenues go up, and they absolutely didn't. We really can't put a handle on that because we don't know what the Oneidas' revenue is."

Barker went on, "We had only one convenience gas station here, and that is gone. We lost a little bit of property tax by [the Oneidas'] refusal to pay. The bigger picture for us is our sales-tax issue. And our state leaders will not collect the sales tax as they are required.

"The Oneidas just went through a $300 million expansion, according to what I read in the papers, and I see the evidence of a lot of it. That is supposedly going to create another 1,000 jobs. It is going to add another $15 million to the payroll in central New York. If you take $15 million and divide it by a thousand, that's $15,000 a job. You know, that is poverty-level. . . . [I]n that 1,000 jobs, there will be some good-paying jobs, but I am talking about an average pay. You cannot raise a family on the majority of jobs that the Oneidas are providing.

"We have talked about taxation, but we have another extremely serious concern, and that is zoning. Our zoning ensures that adjacent uses will be compatible and that property values will be stable. OINNY ignores our zoning. Our people move here, buy homes and businesses, and they have a right to feel secure. What happens if an entity moves in next door to them and you don't know what's going to happen?"

When Barker was asked about any improvements in tourism after the Turning Stone Casino opened, he responded, "The Oneidas tout the fact that they bring in 3 to 4 million visitors a year to central New York, and they do. Their idea is—you come in, you spend your money, we will have 19 restaurants or whatever it is; we will have eight golf courses; we'll have all the things so that you can spend your money right here [at OINNY enterprises]. Then, you get back on the throughway, and we don't want to see you. Or we'll bus you to Syracuse to catch a plane. Our restaurants in Sherrill see little business from the casino. In fact, they are seeing competition from the casino and losing business."

These conversations with David Barker occurred in October 2004. The U.S. Supreme Court had docketed the Sherrill case for oral argument on January 11, 2005. On the city of Sherrill's Web site is its Winter 2005 newsletter issue, which features a lovely photograph of city officials standing in front of the U.S. Supreme Court on January 11, 2005.

No one anticipated a ruling to come down from the Court before May or June 2005. On March 29, however, the news came. The first sentences in the first relevant article published in the *Indian Country Today* newspaper, owned by 4-Directions—an enterprise of the Oneida Indian Nation and its CEO, Halbritter—stated: "Invoking the Doctrine of Discovery, the Supreme Court said repurchased Indian land does not unilaterally revert to tribal sovereign status. In an 8-to-1 ruling, the Court determined that the Oneida Indian Nation of New York cannot unilaterally revive its ancient sovereignty, in whole or in part, over the parcels at issue. The Oneidas long ago relinquished the reins of government and cannot regain them through open-market purchases from current titleholders."

Score One for David

The ruling, by Justice Ruth Bader Ginsburg with a sole dissent from Justice John Paul Stevens, will need months, perhaps years, before its breadth and scope can be fully understood. Several prominent legal counsel and law firms provided extensive pro-bono services to Sherrill, resulting in out-of-pocket cost to the city of only about $100,000 for pursuing the case all the way to the Highest Court.

Several important findings should be noted, as provided in the Court's ruling for *City of Sherrill v. Oneida Indian Nation*:

- "Fee title to the lands occupied by Indians when the colonists arrived became vested in the sovereign—first the discovering European nation and later the original States and the United States." [Doctrine of Discovery]

- "The distance from 1805 to the present day, the Oneidas' long delay in seeking equitable relief against New York or its local units, and developments in Sherrill spanning several generations evoke the doctrines of laches [negligence in asserting a legal right], acquiescence, and impossibility, and render inequitable the piecemeal shift in governance this suit seeks unilaterally to initiate. . . . [T]he doctrine of laches focuses on one side's inaction and the other's legitimate reliance to bar long-dormant claims for equitable relief." [Doctrine of Laches]

- "The long-standing assumption of jurisdiction by the State over an area that is predominantly non-Indian in population and land use creates 'justifiable expectations' . . . [A] contrary conclusion would seriously disrupt the justifiable expectations of the people living in the area." [Acquiescence, Impossibility, Justifiable Expectations]

- "Congress has provided a mechanism for the acquisition of lands for tribal communities that takes account of the interest of others with stakes in the area's governance and well-being. [The law] provides the proper avenue for OINNY to reestablish sovereign authority over territory held by the Oneidas 200 years ago." [Transferring Indian-owned lands from fee [ownership] into federal "trust" status]

Had Sherrill lost the ruling, some 18,000 acres of parcels, mostly noncontiguous in Madison and Oneida counties of New York State, would have been characterized as "Indian country," and removed from the taxable land base. Likewise, the ruling has national implications for tribes that acquire lands outside Indian reservations, an increasing practice since the Indian Gaming Regulatory Act of 1988.

This was a big win for a little town. Credit is well deserved for the leadership of City Manager David Barker, fully supported by the city commission and the entire community.

Reverberations of the Sherrill case have caused the withdrawal of Governor George Pataki's legislation proposing five tribal casinos for Sullivan County, New York. It has called into question the many major Indian land claims encompassing most of upstate and central New York. The ruling may also be an effective tool for communities whose "justifiable expectations" do not include a desire for an encroaching Class III tribal casino.

The Sherrill ruling is a true, much-deserved, and necessary victory for New York's smallest city, especially if, as Barker promises, "our people have expectations and we meet them." They are, for now, less at risk of being parceled into tribal, sovereign "patches" (Justice Ginsburg's word) within an existing local government system. The case will undoubtedly have a substantial impact upon other jurisdictional conflicts arising from federal Indian policy in New York, as well as across the country.

Organizations to Contact

The editors have compiled the following list of organizations concerned with the issues debated in this book. The descriptions are derived from materials provided by the organizations. All have publications or information available for interested readers. The list was compiled on the date of publication of the present volume; the information provided here may change. Be aware that many organizations take several weeks or longer to respond to inquiries, so allow as much time as possible.

Americans for Tax Reform (ATR)
722 Twelfth St. NW, Ste. 400, Washington, DC   20005
(202) 785-0266 • fax: (202) 785-0261
e-mail: info@stopetaxes.com
Web site: www.atr.org

The Americans for Tax Reform (ATR) is a nonprofit organization that believes in a system in which taxes are simpler, flatter, more visible, and lower than they are today. Among other projects, it operates the Web site Stop eTaxes (www. stopetaxes.com), which contains detailed current news about various states' attempts to tax online purchases.

Amish Country News
PO Box 414, Bird-in-Hand, PA   17505
(717) 768-8400, ext. 217
Web site: www.amishnews.com

The Amish Country News is the leading monthly visitor's guide to Amish Country, Lancaster, Pennsylvania, serving as a resource to both visitors and locals wishing to learn more about the Amish. Its Web site contains many articles about the Amish and their way of life, including "The Amish and the IRS," which tells in detail the history of the dispute over payment of Social Security taxes.

Internal Revenue Service (IRS)
1111 Constitution Ave. NW, Washington, DC   20224
(800) 829-1040
Web site: www.irs.gov

The Internal Revenue Service (IRS) is a bureau within the U.S. Treasury that facilitates and enforces citizens' compliance with U.S. tax law. It also provides information about compliance to federal, state, and local governments. The IRS publishes fact sheets, research bulletins, and annual data books.

National Congress of American Indians (NCAI)
1516 P St. NW, Washington, DC   20005
(202) 466-7767 • fax: (202) 466-7797
e-mail: ncai@ncai.org
Web site: www.ncai.org

The National Congress of American Indians (NCAI) is the largest and oldest national Indian organization. It stresses the need for unity and cooperation among tribal governments for the protection of their treaty and sovereign rights. The NCAI filed an *amicus curiae* (friend of the court) brief in *City of Sherrill v. Oneida Indian Nation* and its Web site contains articles related to the case.

Native American Rights Fund (NARF)
506 Broadway, Boulder, CO   80302-6296
(303) 447-8760 • fax: (303) 443-7776
Web site: www.narf.org

Native American Rights Fund (NARF) is a nonprofit organization that provides legal representation and technical assistance to Indian tribes, organizations, and individuals nationwide. Its Web site contains many documents related to the conflict between the Oneida Indians and the City of Sherrill, New York.

Streamlined Sales Tax Governing Board
4205 Hillsboro Pike, Ste. 305, Nashville, TN   37215
(615) 460-9330 • fax: (615) 460-9315

e-mail: jessica.ando@sstgb.org
Web site: www.streamlinedsalestax.org

The goal of the Streamlined Sales Tax Governing Board is to find solutions for the complexity in state sales tax systems that resulted in the U.S. Supreme Court's holdings (in *Bellas Hess v. Illinois* and *Quill Corp. v. North Dakota*) that a state may not require a seller that does not have a physical presence in the state to collect tax on sales into the state. As of 2010 twenty-three states have passed legislation conforming to it. Its Web site contains a FAQ page, the complete agreement, and related documents.

Tax Foundation
National Press Bldg., Washington, DC   20045-1000
(202) 464-6200
e-mail: tf@taxfoundation.org
Web site: www.taxfoundation.org

The mission of the Tax Foundation is to educate taxpayers about sound tax policy and the size of the tax burden borne by Americans at all levels. From its founding in 1937, it has been grounded in the belief that the dissemination of basic information about government finances is the foundation of sound policy in a free society. Its Web site contains many articles about Supreme Court decisions on tax issues.

For Further Research

Books

Stuart Banner, *How the Indians Lost their Land*. Cambridge, MA: Harvard University Press, 2007.

William C. Canby Jr., *American Indian Law in a Nutshell*. St. Paul, MN: West, 2009.

Paul L. Caron, *Tax Stories*. St. Paul, MN: Foundation Press, 2009.

Donald B. Kraybill, ed., *The Amish and the State*. Baltimore: Johns Hopkins University Press, 2003.

Steven L. Pevar, *The Rights of Indians and Tribes*. New York: New York University Press, 2004.

Joseph Francis Zimmerman, *The Silence of Congress: State Taxation of Interstate Commerce*. Albany: State University of New York Press, 2008.

Periodicals

Peter Applebome, "Land, Taxes and a Dispute as Old as the United States," *New York Times*, January 9, 2005.

Associated Press, "U.S. Suggests Trust Plan for Oneida Nation Land," *New York Times*, February 23, 2008.

Dean Brelis, "The Amish and the Law," *Time*, April 19, 1982.

Noam Cohen, "In a State's Search for Sales Tax, Amazon Raises Privacy Concerns," *New York Times*, May 3, 2010.

Charles Cooper, "Beware the Coming Bite: Bureaucrats Pushing New Sales Tax That Would Hike Price of Mail-Order PCs," *Computer Shopper*, April 1992.

Patrice Crowley, "The Sacrament Called Land: To the Amish of Lancaster County, Pennsylvania, Farming Is Akin to Praying," *Country Journal*, May/June 1994.

Steve Forbes, "Fact and Comment," *Forbes*, March 27, 2006.

Geoffrey F. Fowler, "States Pressure e-Tailers to Collect Sales Tax," *Wall Street Journal*, March 18, 2010.

Beverly Gage, "Indian Country, NY," *Nation*, November 27, 2000.

Linda Greenhouse, "Amish Must Pay Social Security Taxes for Their Employees," *New York Times*, February 24, 1982.

———, "Court to Review Mail-Order Sales Tax Curb," *New York Times*, October 8, 1991.

———, "High Court Invites Move by Congress on Mail-Order Tax," *New York Times*, May 27, 1992.

———, "Supreme Court Ruling Supports Tax Protester," *New York Times*, January 9, 1991.

David Cay Johnston, "Mail Order Group Agrees to Collect State Sales Taxes," *New York Times*, November 6, 1997.

Ylan Q. Mui, "Cash-Strapped States Go Online, Hoping to Tax Sales," *Washington Post*, May 2, 2010.

Iver Peterson, "Neighbors See Lesson in Oneida Casino Deal: What Not to Do," *New York Times*, July 30, 2003.

David C. Powell, "Internet Taxation and U.S. Intergovernmental Relations: From *Quill* to the Present," *Publius*, Winter/Spring 2000.

John V. Stevens and John G. Tulio, "Casenote: *United States v. Lee*, a Second Look," *Journal of Church and State*, Summer 1984.

Time, "A Cheeky Defense," January 21, 1991.

Internet Sources

Jim Adams, "Federal Court Rulings Belie Long Struggle," *Indian Country Today*, June 8, 2005. www.indiancountrytoday.com/archive/28165309.html.

————, "Sherrill Hearing Fails to Answer Why Supreme Court Took Case," *Indian Country Today*, January 14, 2005. www.indiancountrytoday.com/archive/28172204.html.

————, "Supreme Court Leaves Ray of Hope After Sherrill Disaster," *Indian Country Today*, June 17, 2005. www.indiancountrytoday.com/archive/28165079.html.

Anti-Defamation League, "Tax Protest Movement," 2005. www.adl.org/learn/ext_us/tpm.asp.

Business Week Online, "The Surge to Impose Online Sales Taxes," April 27, 2009. www.businessweek.com/technology/content/apr2009/tc20090426_510375.htm.

Trisha Kyn Fawler, "Affiliate Marketers to Courts—Kill the Amazon Tax!" *Marketing Pilgrim*, September 12, 2009. www.marketingpilgrim.com/2009/09/affiliate-marketers-to-courts-kill-the-amazon-tax.html.

John Fischer, "SSUTA: Much Ado About Little?" Multichannel Merchant, September 1, 2005. http://multichannel merchant.com/mag/ssuta_ado_little_0901.

Friends Committee on National Legislation, "*City of Sherrill v. Oneida Indian Nation* Supreme Court Decision Goes Against Tribe," April 14, 2005. www.fcnl.org/issues/item.php?item_id=1323&issue_id=94.

Jake Grovum, "The 'Amazon Tax' War Escalates," Stateline, www.stateline.org/live/details/story?contentId=479651.

David Harsanyi, "Harsanyi: Beware the Amazon," *Denver Post*, March 12, 2010. www.denverpost.com/harsanyi/ci_14658950.

Joseph Henchman and Justin Burrows, "'Amazon Tax' Unconstitutional and Unwise," Tax Foundation, September 15, 2009. www.taxfoundation.org/news/show/25120.html.

Huffington Post, "Amazon Reacts to Colorado Internet Sales Tax Measure by Firing Its Colorado Associates," March 8, 2010. www.huffingtonpost.com/2010/03/08/amazon-reacts-to-colorado_n_490028.html.

Indian Country Today, "Will the Indian Dream of the Land Endure?" January 13, 2005. www.indiancountrytoday.com/archive/28172254.html.

Oneida Indian Nation, "Treaty with the Six Nations, 1794," November 6, 2009. www.oneidaindiannation.com/history/69387712.html.

Daniel J. Pilla, "The Untax Promise: Dangerous Tax Schemes That Could Land You in Jail," Tax Help Online, 2001. http://taxhelponline.com/tax-protestor-claims.html.

Roger Russell, "Amazon Tax Case Could Go to Supreme Court," WebCPA, May 7, 2010. www.webcpa.com/news/Amazon-Tax-Case-Could-Hit-Supreme-Court-54139-1.html.

Donny Shaw, "Amish and Other Religious Groups Exempted from the Individual Mandate," OpenCongress Blog, January 11, 2010. www.opencongress.org/articles/view/1448-Amish-and-Other-Religious-Groups-Exempted-from-the-Individual-Mandate.

Wall Street Journal "California Senate Passes So-Called 'Amazon Tax,'" February 19, 2010.

Ryan Young, "How Not to Tax the Internet," *American Spectator Online*, March 24, 2009. http://spectator.org/archives/2009/03/24/how-not-to-tax-the-internet.

Index